# Walk!

# La Gomera

*by*

*Charles Davis*

**DISCOVERY WALKING GUIDES LTD**

**Walk! La Gomera**
**Second Edition** - January 2004
**First published** - August 2000
Copyright © 2004

**Published by**
**Discovery Walking Guides Ltd**
10 Tennyson Close, Northampton NN5 7HJ,
England

**Maps**
Maps are adapted from La Gomera Tour & Trail
Map (Super-Durable Edition, ISBN 1-899554-91-2)
published by **Discovery Walking Guides Ltd**

**Photographs**
Photographs in this book were taken by the author,
Charles Davis, and Jeanette Tallegas. with the
exception of those illustrating Walks 27 and 31,
taken by Ros Brawn.

**Front Cover Photographs**

**Roque Cano**
Walk 29

**Mimbreras,
El Cedro**
Walks 27 & 35

**Imada**
Walks 5
& 12

Charles & Bati
above **Agulo**
Walk 32

ISBN 1-899554-90-4

Text and photographs* © Charles Davis 2004
*Photographs on pages 105 and 113 © Discovery
Walking Guides Ltd.
Maps © David & Ros Brawn

# Walk! La Gomera

## CONTENTS

**WALKS IN THE NORTH** — 101

Charles Davis was born in London, and has lived and worked in the United States, Sudan, Turkey, Ivory Coast, Spain and France. With the onset of middle age, he realised that the urge to roam was better satisfied by walking than bouncing about on the back of a lorry in the middle of the desert, and now divides his time between mountain tops, desk-tops and laptops. He is the author of numerous highly praised and wholly unpublished novels.

Jeanette Tallegas has spent thirty odd years labouring for the French education system, from which she has finally, gleefully, taken early retirement. Asked what she intends doing now, she resolutely replies, "Nothing". Nonetheless, she does follow the author up various gruelling mountains, frequently alarming younger ramblers who seem to assume that remote and inaccessible places are the preserve of youth.

Bati is an Old English Sheepdog. He is large and shaggy and not over-bright. However, he was sufficiently winsome to overcome the author's prejudice against pedigree dogs, and was consequently plucked from the Municipal Dog Pound where he had been dumped by his previous owners. Despite initial misgivings (he expressed a strong preference for staying in the car), he is now quite mad about mountains.

Charles Davis is also the author of:

## 34 Alpujarras Walks

published by Discovery Walking Guides
!SBN 1-899554-83-1

# INTRODUCTION

In 1981, a group of Canadians, anxious to escape the hectic racket of a world made small by noisy machines and modern media, retreated to a remote farm on the isolated and little known islands of…the Falklands. In 1986 in the aftermath of a breathtakingly incompetent experiment at the Chernobyl nuclear power station, the population of La Gomera doubled as ageing German hippies hurried 'home', anxious not to be imbibing radioactive milk and eating day-glo lambs. Guess who made the right choice. La Gomera is the ultimate get-away-from-it-all island, easy-going, unspoilt, friendly, isolated from the hustle and bustle of modern living, and so laid back it's virtually supine - even the volcanoes have been dormant for millions of years, and the Internet seems to operate on a similar time-scale! The walks, however, are a bit more energetic.

## THE ISLAND

Like a large fluted meringue capped with a crown of green icing, La Gomera or The Round Island, would have reduced Roman road-builders to tearful incoherence. There isn't a straight line on the island and the only way to make a road that doesn't wind about like a snake in a pinball machine is to bore a hole through solid rock. The bane of road-builders and blessing for ramblers, are the myriad ravines (*barrancos*) radiating like spokes from the island's central peak, the **Garajonay**, which have militated against attempts to create an elaborate modern infrastructure and obliged generations of shepherds and peasants to trailblaze a network of paths climbing, crossing and circumnavigating a baffling complex of natural obstacles.

There was a theory, long discredited but beguiling nonetheless, that the Canary Islands were the westernmost tip of the Atlas mountains, or even the remains of a broken African peninsula. Certainly, La Gomera looks like some giant scooped up a handful of North Africa and dolloped it down in the middle of the Atlantic. Arriving by boat, the island can seem unforgivingly brown and barren. And yet its ravines cluster round the celebrated *laurisilva* forest of **Garajonay**, arguably the finest remaining example of the woods that covered southern Europe until the last Ice Age.

Though the laurel family predominates, the *laurisilva* is composed of many different species of tree, notably willow and holly, and more plant life than can be catalogued in a chapter, let alone a paragraph. Often compared to a sponge, **Garajonay** epitomises the importance of trees to a living environment, mopping up moisture from the mists brought by the trade winds, and providing as much as half of the island's water supply. Its name comes from a pre-hispanic legend concerning the young lovers, Gara, a Gomeran girl, and Jonay, a boy from Tenerife. Confronted by the customary troubles with elders legendary young lovers generally face, Gara and Jonay took to the mountain and died in one another's arms, speared on a thorn tree. As for the island itself, biblical scholars once claimed it was named for one of Noah's grandsons, Gomer, but a more likely hypothesis is that it's an eponym for early settlers from Mauritania.

## AIM AND SCOPE

This book is aimed at the independent traveller intending to structure a trip round daily walks. There are walks to suit all tastes and capacities, covering all the classic itineraries, in whole or in part, plus several obscure but no less attractive 'new' routes.

## CLIMATE, WHEN TO GO

In summer, only walks in **Garajonay** are practical. Attempt anything down toward the coast and you'll wind up a rambler flavoured crisp. Even in early autumn, the south is too hot for comfortable walking and the magnificent sculpture of its *barrancos* is reduced to an abrasive wilderness that might appeal to religious visionaries, but is likely to have the average hiker hurrying off to hide in the woods. To get the best of the island at all altitudes, late autumn, winter and early spring are the times to go, especially lower down where rocks and shrubs that look shabby and flat under intense sunlight reveal themselves in an extraordinary complexity of form and colour.

## GETTING THERE, GETTING ABOUT, GETTING A BED

There's an **airport** in La Gomera. And there are white elephants in Burma. Since the runway is too short to take any but the most modest modern planes, the principal consequence has been the widening of the road down to **Playa Santiago** and an extension of bus services. Most travellers arrive from Tenerife, on the Fred Olsen fast **ferries**, which run five times a day.

**Hire-car** or **motorbike** is the simplest way of getting about, though a handicap for one-way linear walks. 27 routes are accessible by **bus**, directly, via an extension, or by joining a walk midway (see individual itineraries for details). Three main lines with buses four times a day (see **Appendix B**) serve the principal walking areas with four twice-daily lines linking these routes and more marginal areas. Timetables rarely change, but call at the Tourist Office for up-to-date information. The aqua coloured *Servicio Regular* buses are public. Other companies are for private coach parties. **Taxi** drivers are used to dropping people off at the start of more popular routes, though this is a comparatively expensive option. A **local ferry** company, Garajonay Exprés, has departures three times a day linking **San Sebastián**, **Playa Santiago** and **Valle Gran Rey**, providing a cheap and agreeable option to the buses.

**Accommodation** in hotels, pensions, apartments and *casas rurales* is plentiful and geared to independent travellers rather than block-booking packages. The walks are evenly spread and, since the island is small, accessible wherever you maybe staying, so **choosing a base** is a question of taste rather than practicality. **San Sebastián** is best for bus routes, with **Valle Gran Rey** a close second. The facilities in each are comparable, though **Valle Gran Rey** has a slight edge in terms of tourist-centred services. **Playa Santiago** and **Valle Gran Rey** are as 'touristy' as it gets on **La Gomera**, though food shops in the former are poor. Both are good if you want a bathe at the end of a day's walking. **Hermigua** and **Vallehermoso** perhaps boast the best balance between facilities, affordability and an authentically Gomeran atmosphere. Tranquility seekers should check out the *Casas Rurales*. If time allows, it's worth spending three or four days in each area, in which case contact one of the agencies dealing with *casas rurales, viviendas,* and *apartamentos*. See **Appendix A** for addresses and recommendations.

## THE WALKS

One unfortunate consequence of having so many ravines is that Canarians have a regrettable tendency to build roads right over the top of their highest mountains, which is all very well for conventional tourists, but a bit dispiriting for ramblers. Getting somewhere one can't otherwise go is, after all, one of the great pleasures of walking and it's a bit galling to get to the top, lungs gasping, legs wobbly, T-shirt sodden and heart lodged somewhere round the back of your oesophagus, only to find yourself on a main road with a regular bus service. Hence the linear descents. Nonetheless, exceptional circuits demand exceptional efforts, so I make my excuses in advance, first for the logistical hassles of those walks involving public transport at both ends, second for itineraries that have you toiling up a mountain only to be met by a coach load of baffled tourists wondering why you didn't take the package.

All the walks *are* walks and require no special **equipment** or **expertise**, with the exception of Walk 34, on which a torch is essential. Otherwise, all you need are walking boots or tough walking sandals, and protection appropriate to the weather and altitude. In the **Garajonay** it's advisable always to have a waterproof and/or light sweater. At lower altitudes, a sun hat and sun cream are essential. Within each section, the first walk is suitable as a **test walk** for the first day. The remaining walks are arranged according to a vaguely geographical logic, not by difficulty or length.

There is no uniform system of **waymarking** on La Gomera and each local authority has its own style of signpost – or not as the case may be! There are two unofficial GRs (*Gran Recorrido* or long-distance walks with red-and-white **waymarks)** forking out from **San Sebastián** to **Playa Santiago** and **Hermigua**. PR (*Pequeño Recorrido*, short walks) signposts are appearing in **Vallehermoso** and SL (*Sendero Local*, local footpath) signs around **Cercado** and **Chipude**, but there are no waymarks to date. PRs are conventionally waymarked yellow-and-white, SLs green-and-white. The most coherent system of signboards are found in the **Garajonay** National Park.

**Timings** are all 'pure' timings excluding snacking, snapping and simply standing still staring. It's highly unlikely you will complete these walks in exactly the time specified. Try a shorter walk first to see how your times compare to mine. As a rule of thumb, add fifteen minutes to every timed hour. But above all, take YOUR time. There's nothing more frustrating than trying to walk at somebody else's pace, be it slower or faster than yours. Similarly, all assessments of **exertion** are subjective and are bound to vary according to personal prejudice, general temperament and the mood of the day. You can be fairly sure that, somewhere along the line, you'll be cursing me for a pathetic weed or a macho maniac. Apologies!

I've tried to give enough detail in the **descriptions** for those who need confirmation they're on the right path, but not so much as to irritate more confidant pathfinders with superfluity. *Italics* are used for discrete Spanish words, most of which are found in the glossary, and single quotes indicate a place name written on a signpost. **Bold Text** is used for place names, including named geographic features, and also for street names and the names of bars and businesses encountered on the walks. Consistency rather than deficient vocabulary accounts for all **ascents and descents** being 'gentle', 'steady', or 'steep'.

As a general guide a **dirt track** or *pista forestal* indicates something that could be driven, albeit sometimes at a pinch, a **trail** refers to something reasonably broad but better suited to feet, hooves or two wheels rather than four, a **path** is a path, and a **way** either aspires to being a path or was once a path and has long since given up an unequal battle with erosion and/or vegetation. To link more interesting paths, road walking is sometimes inevitable. No road on the island is really big or busy, so don't be alarmed by references to **main roads**, most of which would be considered bucolically peaceful in Britain. As for what I call **lanes**, they are frequently little more than tracks with a barrow load of tarmac tipped on top and smeared about a bit.

## RISKS

Aggressive **dogs**, disagreeable **landowners**, and **theft** are not a problem. **Forest fires** are a danger in summer and early autumn. **Dehydration** is the most prevalent risk, especially at lower altitudes. Take half a litre of water per person per hour and bear in mind that dehydration affects the entire body, including joints and tendons. If you suspect your knees might come in handy in thirty years' time, drink plenty before descending. **Swimming** can be dangerous, especially in the north and west. As a general rule, don't swim unless you see other people getting in and, more importantly, getting out.

## FLORA & FAUNA

The **Garajonay** Park Visitors' Guide claims 980 plant species and subspecies exist on La Gomera (there's 27 species of ferns alone!), which makes one short paragraph look a little silly, but to give you a rough idea of what to expect, the following observations (and they are observations, what we noticed, not what a professional eye might discern) may serve as a rough introduction. Bear in mind that anything liable to be a shrub in continental Europe will be a bush here, while familiar bushes take on the dimension of trees, the obvious example being the heath-tree or *brezo.*

The first thing you'll notice are palm trees, which are so prevalent the fronds assume the same function broom used to in Britain. In drier areas you will see plenty of prickly pear (often spotted with the flaky white parasite from which cochineal was extracted), agave, wax-plants, fennel, St. John's wort, spurge, house-leeks, sow-thistle, taginaste, bugloss, cistus, tansy, several types of daisy and more varieties of broom than you can shake a palm frond at. The real glory of the island's flora though is to be found in the green crown of **Garajonay**. In the text, I use *laurisilva* loosely as shorthand for the **Garajonay** woods, though inevitably the flora, even of superficially similar woodland, is more complex than this suggests. In drier areas the correct term is *fayal-brezal*, a composite of the Spanish words for wax-myrtle and tree-heath. To get an idea of how rich this forest is, go to the **Centro de Visitantes** near **Las Rosas** and ask for the park's free pamphlet of Self-Guider Paths, which details three short itineraries, two of them covered in stretches of Walks 13,14 & 35 and one, **Los Barranquillos** (north of **Arure**), too short to count as a described itinerary, but a pleasant stroll for a day-off.

By comparison, La Gomera seems relatively poor in fauna. The odd hoopoe may brighten your day and there are numerous varieties of finches and tits, otherwise the most common birds are turtle doves, kestrels and hawks. There are said to be 2000 species of insect on the island, the most eye-catching being the dragonflies, which are remarkably varied, not just electric blue but pale blue and, most startlingly, scarlet. Apart from rabbits and partridge, there is no game on La Gomera. The most common reptile is the Gomeran lizard, a dark-skinned, antediluvian looking creature usually seen belting about in the crevices of rocks. You may also see the coppery backed *lisa*, which resembles a slow-worm with legs.

## EATING AND DRINKING

Possibly the most distinctive dish on La Gomera is cress soup (*sopa de berros*), which is on most menus. More of a broth than a soup, it's an ideal walkers'meal, filling but not sleep inducing. The other characteristic ingredient of local cuisine, found throughout the Canaries but particularly popular here, is maize meal or *gofio*. If you're presented with a saltshaker or bowl of beige flour, it's *gofio* and you're expected to sprinkle it on your soup. Otherwise, standard Canary cuisine prevails, which is to say meat (*carne*) and potatoes (*patatas* or *papas*) with lashings of *mojo*, a sauce variously made of red (*mojo rojo*) or green peppers and coriander (*mojo verde*) – and very various it is, too, everybody boasting their own recipe which is inevitably better than everyone else's.

Meat is *asado* (which on the mainland means roast but here sometimes means braised), *a la plancha* (griddled), *a la brasa* (barbecued), *frita* (fried), or *con salsa* (stewed). *Cabra* is goat, *cerdo* pork, *buey, ternera* or *res* beef, and *cordero* lamb. Notable specialities are *cabra con salsa* and *carne fiesta*, fried marinated pork. Potatoes are 'wrinkled' (*papas arrugados*), which is to say boiled in their jackets with lots of salt and little water, resulting in a taste and texture that suggests parboiling and baking. They tend to be cooked early and left to stand, so don't be surprised if they're lukewarm. Pulses are not as common as elsewhere in Spain, though chick peas (*garbanzos*) are ubiquitous, often as a labourer's mid-morning 'snack', and you may see beans (*judias*) or lentils (*lentejas*).

Fish (*pescado*) is not so widespread as one would expect either, though tuna (*atun*) is on most menus. Salad is nearly always the standard mix (*ensalada mixta*). Asking for cheese (*queso*) you will be given a choice of white (*blanco*) or yellow (*amarillo*), the former being the local goat's cheese, the latter a limp sheet of plastic imported from the mainland. *Almogrote* is a piquant pâté of grated cheese, garlic and peppers – only worthwhile if freshly prepared; avoid the potted gunge sold in supermarkets and tourist shops.

The local beers (*cerveza*), Dorada, Reina, and Tropical, are additive free and good. Most of the island's viniculture is destined for private rather than commercial use, but Gomeran red and white (mostly the latter) wines are available and, with names like Garajonay and Roque Cano, readily identifiable. They're not great, but good enough. Of the whites, Asocado is the best and Garajonay is better than Montoro, despite, or perhaps because of the latter's eye-catchingly archaic label. *Gomeron* is the local hooch and *Mistella* is the same stuff cut with spiced wine. Finally, you may notice locals being served coffee with a sludge of condensed milk lurking about at the bottom of the glass. This is a *barraquito*. Occasionally the condensed milk is diluted with ordinary milk and sometimes, bizarrely but not unpleasantly, a shaving of lemon rind is added for flavour.

## TOURIST STUFF

La Gomera is refreshingly free of the compulsion to be constantly grabbing your attention and extracting wads of money from your wallet, which means there is little to excite the conventional tourist apart from the views. If you have a chance to see and hear something of *silbo*, the island's ancient whistling language, it's worth taking the opportunity. If you want a day off walking but don't want to be stuck indoors, the *ermitas* make good **picnic spots**, notably **San Juan** at **Benchijigua** (see Walks 7&9), **Nuestra Señora de Guadalupe** above **Gerián** (see Walks 21 & 22), **San Salvador** in **Taguluche** (see Walk 26), **San Isidro** at the **Chorros de Epina** (see Walk 30), **Santa Clara** (see Walk 30, driveable dirt track), **Lourdes** (see Walk 35) and **Las Nieves** on the TF713.

Playa del Medio

Best **beaches** for an afternoon lazing around in the sun and swimming are **Las Salinas**, south of **Valle Gran Rey**, and **Playa del Medio** east of **Playa Santiago**. If you want a swim and don't fancy the waves and murky water of the northern beaches, the pool at **Playa de Vallehermoso** is highly recommended (open 12-8, no charge).

Scuba **diving** is possible from **Playa Santiago** and **Valle Gran Rey**. For those who want to be on the water rather than in it, there's the Garajonay Exprés commuter ferry or, the one undisputed non-pedestrian tourist attraction on the island, a **boat trip** from **Valle Gran Rey** to the cliffs of **Los Organos**, an excursion that may also include whale-watching.

## ACKNOWLEDGEMENTS

After three books, the thanks are becoming customary, but no less heartfelt: to Jeannette for company, encouragement, care and persuading me to take a day off once in a while; to Ros and David Brawn for suggesting the book and sharing their invaluable expertise on the island; to Bati for totally disregarding what looked like decidedly creaky hips; and to the Gomerans for giving the lie to common definitions of 'insularity'.

our rating for effort/exertion:-
**1** very easy     **2** easy     **3** average
**4** energetic     **5** strenuous

approximate **time** to complete a walk (compare your times against ours early in a walk) - does not include stopping time

approximate walking **distance** in kilometres

approximate **ascents/descents** in metres (N = negligible)

**circular** route

**linear** route

risk of **vertigo**

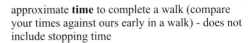

**refreshments** (may be at start or end of a route only)

Find information on how to access walks by bus and/or by ferry (if available) at the start of each walk description.

Bus and ferry timetables can be found in Appendix B. Please note that timetables are subject to change; check in the Tourist Offices, Ferry Offices or bus station in San Sebastián on arrival for up to date information.

Walk descriptions include:

- timing in minutes, shown as (40M)

- compass directions, shown as (NW)

- heights in metres, shown as (1355m)

- GPS waypoints, shown as (Wp.3)

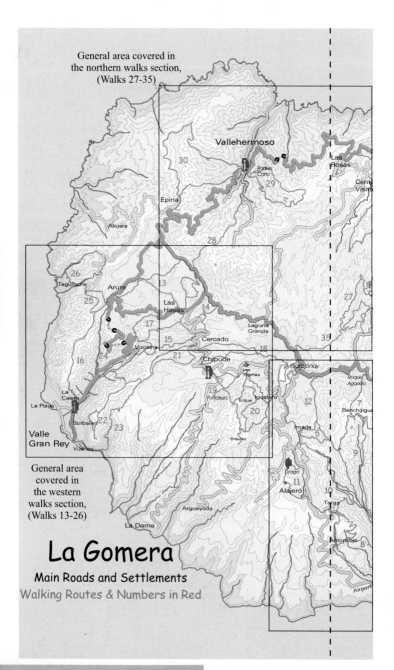

General area covered in
the northern walks section,
(Walks 27-35)

Vallehermoso

Las Rosas

Centro
Visita

30

Roque
Cano

29

Epina

Alojera

28

26

Taguluche

25

Arure

3

Las
Hayas

14

27

E
C

17

Laguna
Grande

33

15

Cercado

18

16

24

Vizcaina

21

Chipude

Garajonay

Roque
Agando

Las
Hejortas

12

7

Benchijigua

19

Fortaleza

Erque

Igualero

La Calera

La Playa

Borbalan

22

20

Imada

9

23

Erquito

Valle
Gran Rey

Vueltas

General area
covered in
the western
walks section,
(Walks 13-26)

Drago

11

Alajeró

10

Targa

Arguayoda

La Dama

Antoncojo

8

# La Gomera

### Main Roads and Settlements

Walking Routes & Numbers in Red

Airport

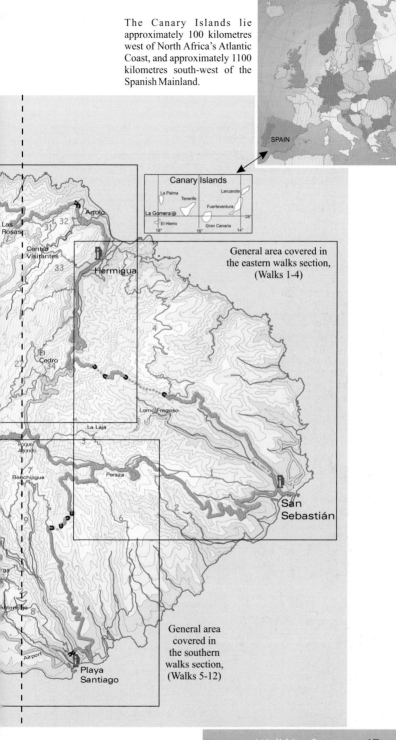

The Canary Islands lie approximately 100 kilometres west of North Africa's Atlantic Coast, and approximately 1100 kilometres south-west of the Spanish Mainland.

SPAIN

Canary Islands

La Palma
Tenerife
Lanzarote
La Gomera
Fuerteventura
El Hierro
Gran Canaria

General area covered in the eastern walks section, (Walks 1-4)

Agulo
Las Rosas
Centro Visitantes
Hermigua
El Cedro
Lomo Fragoso
La Laja
Taguel Alajeró
Benchijigua
Peraza
San Sebastián
Antoncojo
Airport
Playa Santiago

General area covered in the southern walks section, (Walks 5-12)

The map sections used in this book have been adapted from **La Gomera Tour & Trail Super-Durable Map** published by Discovery Walking Guides Ltd. In the interests of clarity, not all waypoints referred to in the walk descriptions are shown in the map sections.

**La Gomera Tour & Trail Super-Durable Map** is a 1:40,000 full colour map. For more information on DWG publications, write to DWG Ltd., 10 Tennyson Close, Northampton NN5 7HJ, England, or visit:

**www.walking.demon.co.uk     www.dwgwalking.co.uk**

## ALTITUDE, HÖHE, ALTITUD, ALTITUDE

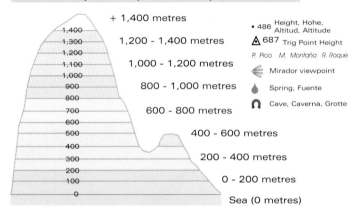

+ 1,400 metres

1,200 - 1,400 metres

1,000 - 1,200 metres

800 - 1,000 metres

600 - 800 metres

400 - 600 metres

200 - 400 metres

0 - 200 metres

Sea (0 metres)

• 486  Height, Hohe, Altitud, Altitude

A 687  Trig Point Height

P. Pico  M. Montaña  R. Roque

Mirador viewpoint

Spring, Fuente

Cave, Caverna, Grotte

## ROADS, STRAßE, CARRETERA, ROUTE

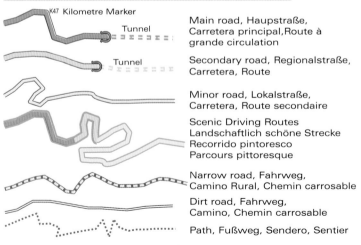

K47 Kilometre Marker

Tunnel — Main road, Hauptstraße, Carretera principal, Route à grande circulation

Tunnel — Secondary road, Regionalstraße, Carretera, Route

Minor road, Lokalstraße, Carretera, Route secondaire

Scenic Driving Routes Landschaftlich schöne Strecke Recorrido pintoresco Parcours pittoresque

Narrow road, Fahrweg, Camino Rural, Chemin carrosable

Dirt road, Fahrweg, Camino, Chemin carrosable

Path, Fußweg, Sendero, Sentier

## Walking Routes, Wanderweg, Sendero, Chemin.

Walk La Gomera Route (Red)

17   GPS Waypoint
see Waypoint Lists

Major Hotel   Important House, Casa Major   Hotel   Petrol

Forestry House, Casa Forestal   House, Casa   Ruin/Barn

Lighthouse, Leuchtturm, Faro, Phare   Bar/Rest

Tower, Turm, Torre, Tour   Information Office   P Parking, Parkplatz

Church, Kirche, Iglesia, Église   Chapel, Kapelle, Ermita, Chapelle

Picnic area, Rastplatz, Zona Recreativa, Pique-nique

Cemetery, Friedhof, Cementario, Cimetière

Sports Ground, Sportplatz, Campo deportivo, Terrain de sport

Camping, Campingplatz, Camping, Camping

Wind Turbine, Windkraftwerk, Eólica, Éolienne

The GPS Waypoint lists provided in this all-new second edition of **Walk!
La Gomera** guide book by Charles Davis, are as recorded by Charles
during his research of the 35 main walk descriptions contained in the book,
although in the interests of clarity not all waypoints included in these lists
are shown on the maps which accompany each detailed walk description.
Where a Waypoint symbol is shown on a map it has been placed alongside
the position it refers to so as to not obscure the map detail.

For readers wondering what we are talking about, the GPS Waypoints are
also Grid References to the exact locations within each walking route when
used in conjunction with the **La Gomera Tour & Trail Super-Durable
Map**.

All The GPS Waypoints quoted in Walk! La Gomera, and on the Tour &
Trail Map, were recorded during the research of the walking routes and are
subject to the general considerations as to the accuracy of GPS units in the
location concerned. It is virtually impossible to reproduce the exact GPS
Waypoint co-ordinates in practice when walking a route. While GPS
Waypoints are quoted to 00.0001 minutes of arc, in practice you should
expect 10 metres as an acceptable standard of accuracy when you have '3D
navigation' (four or more satellites in view).

**Signal Strength**
Signal strength from sufficient satellites is crucial to obtaining an accurate
location fix with your GPS unit. In open sky, ridge top, conditions you may
have up to 11 satellites in view to give you a GPS location accuracy of 5
metres. However, La Gomera is famous for its deep gorges (*barrancos*) and
dense Laurel forest (a UNESO world heritage site), and in these regions
GPS accuracy is compromised by 'mountain shadowing' and the bulk of the
tree trunks blocking satellite signals resulting in intermittent '3D GPS
Location'. Even where you appear to have good satellite reception, it could
be you are receiving reflected signals from a nearby cliff face.

Most of the time your GPS will perform wonderfully, giving you an
accurate location fix, but routes subject to poor GPS reception include 13,
14, 27, 34 and 35 in the Garajonay forest.

**To Input the Waypoints**
GPS Waypoint co-ordinates are quoted for the WGS84 datum, used to
provide grid references on the Tour & Trail Map, in degrees and minutes of
Latitude and Longitude. To input the Waypoints into your GPS we suggest
that you:

- switch on your GPS and select 'simulator' mode.
- check that your GPS is set to the WGS84 datum (its default datum) and
  the 'location format' 'hddd° .mm.mmm'.
- input the GPS Waypoints into a 'route' file with the same number as the
  walking route number; then when you call up the 'route' on La Gomera
  there will be no confusion as to which walking route it refers to.
- repeat the inputting of routes until you have covered all the routes you

plan to walk, or until you have used up the memory capacity of your GPS; even the most basic of GPS units will store up to 20 routes of up to 50 Waypoints for each route, and you can always re-programme your GPS while on La Gomera.

- turn off your GPS. When you turn the GPS back on it should return to its normal navigation mode.

GPS Waypoints are provided as an additional navigation aid to complement the detailed walk descriptions in Walk! La Gomera. Knowing exactly where you are in relation to our detailed walk description is a great confidence booster when exploring these new and exciting landscapes. GPS Waypoints are provided for all key navigational points on all walking routes; never again should you find yourself wondering whether you are on the right path or not.

Note that GPS Waypoints complement the detailed walking route descriptions in Walk La Gomera; they should not be used as an alternative to the detailed walking route description.

**Confused by GPS?**
If you are confused by talk of GPS, but are interested in how this modern navigational aid could enhance your walking enjoyment then simply seek out a copy of **GPS The Easy Way**, the UK's best selling GPS manual. Written in an easy to read, lively, style and lavishly illustrated 'GPS The Easy Way' takes you through all aspects of GPS usage from absolute basics up to GPS Expert and debunking the myths about GPS along the way; an essential purchase for anyone thinking of buying a GPS.

"A compass points north"
but
"A GPS tells you where you are, where you have been, and can show you where you want to go."

"Ask not 'What is GPS?' - ask 'What can GPS do for me?' "

**GPS The Easy Way** is available from bookshops, outdoor shops, over the internet, and post free from:

Discovery Walking Guides Ltd.
10 Tennyson Close
Northampton NN5 7HJ

# WALKING EQUIPMENT

Reading the postings on uk.rec.walking internet news group, it is obvious that walkers are very interested in the clothing and equipment used by other walkers. For some this interest borders on obsession, with heated debates over walking poles, boots versus sandals, GPS versus 'map and compass' navigation etc etc. Walking magazines are packed with clothing and equipment reviews, opinions and adverts, but few walking guide books give more than a cursory mention to recommended clothing and equipment. At the risk of upsetting some walking fundamentalists, here is a brief rundown on what I've used on La Gomera.

## Backpack

A 25-30 litre day pack should easily cope with all the equipment you think you will need for a day's walking. A design with plenty of outside pockets to give easy access to frequently used items, such as ½ litre water bottles, is a good starting point. Well padded straps will spread the load and a waist strap will stop the pack moving about on the more adventurous routes. A ventilated back panel will help clear sweat on hot days and tough routes; a design with a stand-off frame is best for ventilation and worth the small increase in weight. Do spend time adjusting the straps so that you get the most comfortable fit.

As an alternative to traditional backpack designs, you might find the cyclist's packs produced by Nikko, and similar companies, a good compromise of stand-off frame, capacity, pockets and weight.

## Footwear

La Gomera's dramatic landscapes offer no compromises, and nor should you compromise on your footwear. While there are many comfortable paths on the island, a lot of the walking is on hard rock, usually uneven. Whether you choose boots, shoes or sandals they must be up to the task. You will need a hard sole with plenty of grip and a well padded foot-bed. My favourites are a pair of Bestard boots that I picked up at their factory shop on Mallorca. Worn with thick mountain socks, these boots have done everything I have asked of them.

Whichever footwear you choose, do make sure that you have covered plenty of kilometres in them before coming to La Gomera.

## Sun Protection

Always carry a comfortable sun hat, also useful should it rain. Choose a design that gives you plenty of shade, is comfortable to wear, and stays on your head in windy conditions. You will be spending several hours a day outdoors and sunburnt ears (and neck) are both painful and embarrassing. Sunglasses and high-factor sun cream are highly recommended.

## Water & Food

Always carry as much water as you think you might drink. A couple of ½ litre bottles, a few pence each from local shops, is the minimum, and add another couple of litres for routes such as Walk 20, Barranco de Erque. Even on shorter routes, I would advise that you carry some survival rations. While some routes are well equipped with 'tipico' bars many of these are shut on Mondays and survival rations of chocolate bars and the like can provide welcome comfort.

## Medical Kit

Antiseptic wipes, antiseptic cream, plasters and bandage are supplemented by lip salve, which can seem like a life saver in hot dry conditions. Also include tweezers, which you will soon appreciate if you catch a splinter or cactus spine, and a whistle to attract attention if you get into difficulties.

## Navigation

Do not compromise - buy the best guide book and the best map, and carry them with you. A compass is useful to orientate yourself at the start of a route and for general directions, but a GPS unit is far more useful - see Using GPS on La Gomera.

## Clothing

Choose loose comfortable clothing and add a lightweight waterproof jacket to your back pack; the Canary Islands are famous for sunshine but I saw quite a bit of rain while researching this book.

## Other Equipment

You won't want to be carrying excess weight during your walking, especially on the longer routes with major ascents/descents. Digital cameras weigh far less than their film equivalents, and a monocular is half the weight of a pair of binoculars. Secateurs might seem an unusual choice of walking equipment, but they were particularly useful on Walk 31, Las Rosas - Hermigua. A mobile phone, and money (refreshments, taxis, public telephones, drinks machines etc.) are also recommended.

# THE EAST - COMMERCE AND ABANDONMENT

Arriving by ferry from Los Cristianos gives you your first view of La Gomera, the boat's size seeming to dominate the island's capital as it manoeuvres into the small port. Many visitors miss **San Sebastián** all together as they are bussed off around the new roads to the south and west of the island, but this is their loss. Nestling between the new roads and the cliffs, the capital is a maze of almost traffic-free streets bustling with commerce. Here is the island's shopping and commercial centre, along with a wide range of bars and restaurants, a helpful tourist office, and the island's bus station.

You will still find a wide range of tourist accommodation, ranging from the impressive but rather soulless Parador down to hostels and guest houses, but as **San Sebastián** has grown commercially, it has also declined as a tourist destination. Frequent ferry departures mean that business travellers no longer have to overnight in the capital, while vastly improved roads hasten tourists away to the growing resorts of **Valle Gran Rey** and **Playa Santiago**. While the majority of visitors bypass the town, **San Sebastián** can be a good base for drivers craving the sedate grandeur of the Parador and non-drivers combining the bus routes with the nearest you will find to lively nightlife.

It is decades since people swopped the struggle of farming for the suits and overalls of commerce, so returning much of the land back to nature. The relatively barren ridges above the **Barranco de la Villa** and **Barranco Hondo** valleys have a brooding, enigmatic air which you can experience on Walks 1 & 2, while for a short walk follow route 2 out to **Playa de la Guancha**.

**San Sebastián** still trades on its Christopher Columbus connection, with a small tower which seems to always be shut, but the town's most recent tourist success is the bustling yacht marina which has attracted sailors from Tenerife, and further afield, to base their yachts here; the combination of maritime town and good harbour making for one of the best yachting bases in the Canary Islands.

# 1. DEGOLLADA DE PERAZA - SAN SEBASTIÁN

A useful 'commuting' route for those piecing together a long distance walking tour and a fine excursion in itself on a blustery but dry winter's day, this itinerary follows the remains of a traditional donkey trail, precursor to the current road. Not recommended when hot or wet. Though downhill, it gets a high exertion rating as the way is often rough.

**Access**: by bus 🚌 L1 or L2. *in San Sebastián

🚢 If you're staying in **Valle Gran Rey** or **Playa Santiago** this would be a good route to combine with a return trip on the Garajonay Exprés ferry.

From the **Degollada de Peraza** bus-stop (Wp.1, 0M), we follow the **San Sebastián** road (E), ignoring a dirt track on the left immediately after the **Peraza** bar. 400 metres from the bus-stop, we turn left into a fenced compound below the antenna-topped peak of **Tagamiche** (Wp.2, 5M). Crossing the compound, we pass in front of two white buildings. Immediately after the second building, we leave the compound and the main **Tagamiche** track, bearing right on an abandoned track obscured by a bank of thistles. The track dwindles to a path before widening again as it curves to the east of **Tagamiche**. After passing under telephone cables, it runs into a U-bend, where we have a choice of routes, one off-path and picturesque, the other simpler but with slightly less attractive views.

### For the picturesque route

We branch left before the U-bend on a narrow path marked with a tiny red dot on a rock (Wp.3 15M). The path ends at an old wall next to another red-dotted rock, but maintaining direction (NE), we recover faint traces of a way heading toward a palm tree, shortly before which we bear left at a fork. Descending across terraces (ENE), we skirt a precipitous escarpment, crossing a succession of stone walls and outcrops of rock before picking our way through a maze of rocks down to a roofless ruin (invisible till we're almost on top of it) in a large grove of palms (Wp.4 25M). Maintaining an easterly direction, we pass the pitted block of the 862 metre summit, where our faint 'way' disappears in a shelf of rock. Bearing slightly right, towards the road (SSE), we descend across terraces to another ruin, 30 metres below which, we turn left on a clear, cobbled, donkey trail (Wp.5 35M).

### For the easy route

We continue through the U-bend and, immediately after passing back under the telephone cables, turn left onto the start of the intermittently cobbled donkey trail. The trail crosses a small rise and descends (NNE), passing behind two roofless ruins and below a third, which is where we are joined by the picturesque route (Wp.5 30M, 10M from Wp.6).

"..fine views of the conical Roque Sombrero.."

Climbing to the right of a white seam of rock, the donkey trail skirts the southern side of the diminutive, table-top **Pico Gomera**, with fine views of the conical **Roque Sombrero** (see Walk 2). Passing below **Pico Gomera**, we bear left at a first Y-junction (Wp.6 45M) and right at a second (Wp.7 50M), staying on the main cobbled trail.

Large flat rocks replace the cobbles as we approach the first of the **Ayamosna** farms, where we ignore terraces studded with cairns that appear to be waymarkers but are in fact boundary stones. Sticking to the donkey trail, we run alongside a rough tarmac lane, which we join in front of two farmhouses. After 50 metres, we come to a junction (Wp,8 65M) five metres to the left of which, we leave the tarmac and recover the donkey trail. Ignoring a rough branch to the right just before a transformer hut, we pass below the third **Ayamosna** farm, after which we see the quay in **San Sebastián**.

The trail descends behind two partially interred bunkers, of sufficient ugliness to suggest total burial might have been preferable, where it appears to branch left along a terrace dotted with blue painted rocks (Wp.9 80M). In fact, we continue alongside the fence to the left of the bunkers, also passing to the left of the next electricity pylon, after which we join a dirt track (Wp.10 90M). When the track swings sharp right 100 metres later, we continue straight ahead (E) on a narrow shortcut path, a procedure repeated at the next sharp bend (Wp.11 100M). Passing a large ruin, the track swings north-east to approach a row of shabby bungalows, just before which we turn right, leaving the track and recovering the donkey trail (Wp.12 105M).

Zigzagging down a long *lomo* amid a sea of house-leeks, the trail becomes slightly obscure. Ignoring all dirt paths, notably at Wp.13 (120M), we stick to the cobbled way, first on the southern flank of the *lomo* then on the northern flank, eventually descending below a water hut to a rough terrace on the fringes of **San Sebastián** (Wp.14 140M). The terrace runs into a turning circle at the end of **Avenida de las Galanas**, at the bottom of which we turn left into **Calle Isla de Gran Canaria**, then right to descend to the bridge into town (Wp.15 150M).

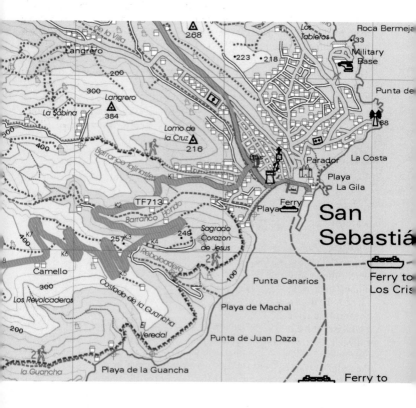

# 2. ROQUE SOMBRERO & PLAYA DE LA GUANCHA

If you only have time to do one walk in the east, this is the one to do. Following a long ridge studded with *roques*, notably the distinctively conical **Sombrero**, it's every bit as wild and exciting as it looks from the road, possibly a little more. A word of warning, though. The main descent is little frequented and, though never difficult, requires considerable confidence, not to mention stamina, as we follow negligible paths in very isolated countryside.

5    4H 40M    16 km    300m / 1300m    4*

*in San Sebastián

**Access**: by bus L1 or L2

**Short Version**
San Sebastian – Playa de la Guancha
(see text for access)

We start as per Walk 1 (taking the easy route; you'll get 'picturesque' later!), but <u>turn right</u> at Wp.8 (60M) and follow the **Ayamosna** access lane to the main road. Crossing the road, we slip between the concrete and metal crash barriers directly ahead of us (Wp.1 65M), as indicated by a red dot on the metal barrier, and take a roughly paved trail into **Barranco de la Guancha**. The trail soon dwindles to a dirt path descending (W) to a flat spur, where we bear right, crossing a watershed and, just beyond a clump of invasive agave, the ravine's main watercourse (Wp.2 80M)

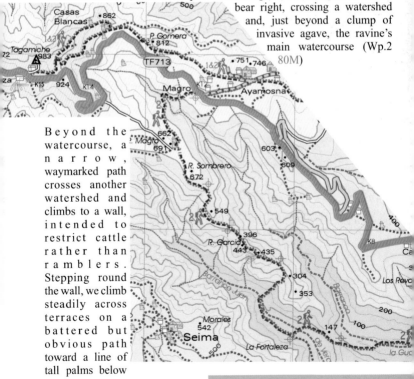

Beyond the watercourse, a narrow, waymarked path crosses another watershed and climbs to a wall, intended to restrict cattle rather than ramblers. Stepping round the wall, we climb steadily across terraces on a battered but obvious path toward a line of tall palms below

**Roque Magro**. The path gets fainter toward the top and the main route to the **Roque Magro** hamlet, though evident from the road, is less apparent on the ground. We can either maintain direction to pick our way along the path or (as mapped) bear left on a cairn-marked terrace and pass <u>below</u> the palms, where a faint trodden way leads to a corner post in a wire mesh fence. Squeezing between the fence and the terrace wall, we follow the terrace until we see the first of the **Roque Magro** ruins. Bearing right, we climb directly across the terraces to the lower ruin, where another terrace curves round to a faint dirt path (Wp.3 100M) crossing the saddle behind **Roque Sombrero**.

Skirting to the right of **Roque Sombrero**, with fine views over **Barranco Juan de Vera**, we cross a rough barrier of agave-scapes and another wall, then follow a raised path toward the nameless, 549 metre *roque* (hereafter referred to as '**549**'), getting our first glimpse of the coastal oasis of **El Cabrito**. After a small windbreak (Wp.4 115M), the path loses definition in rough yellow rocks. Staying on top of the ridge, we pick our way through the rocks toward **549**, passing to the right of a long outcrop of grey rock. At a junction 40 metres before **549** (Wp.5 120M), we fork right on a roughly paved way intermittently defined by low retaining walls. Crossing a thin plastic pipe, we wind down through palm trees onto a clearer dirt path below the fluted cliffs of **549**. After passing a large '4' daubed on the rock, we emerge on a broad saddle at a solitary palm (Wp.6 130M) between a ruin and a rock with '2' painted on it.

Ahead of us are the three distinct *roques* known collectively as **Roque Garcia**. Crossing the saddle, we climb to the right of the smaller, central *roque*, after which we bear right then immediately left (ESE) on a broad ledge running between the easternmost *roque* and a precipitous slope. At the end of the ledge, we climb past a partially walled cave onto a crocodile back spur from where **El Cabrito** is visible again (Wp.7 140M). Continuing alongside the ridge, we descend to a narrow spine distinguished by a 3-metre rock 'hand' (Wp.8 145M) - admittedly a somewhat freakish and mutilated hand, but a hand nonetheless- just after which, we see a green-and-white waymark.

From here a direct descent into **Barranco de la Guancha** would be possible and even describable, but it would also be pathless and I suspect undesirable. Instead, we follow the green-and-white waymarked route, winding down into **Barranco Juan de Vera**, where we cross the riverbed and join the end of a dirt track (Wp.9 165M). To return to **Barranco de la Guancha**, we will re-cross the ridge at its lowest point, just before the pylon we can see to the east. The track drops down into a wide bend of the riverbed, where you may see cairns and a solitary green-and-white waymark to the left. These indicate an alternative way up to Wp.11, but after 15 minutes fruitless boulder-hopping, I failed to find it! Far simpler to follow the dirt track till you come to a cross-roads with a path, a metal sign indicating *Seima* to the right and a flurry of cairns and red-and-white waymarks tracing our route across the riverbed to the left (Wp.10 170M).

Turning left, we follow the abundant waymarks and cairns across the river to a rough dirt and rock path climbing gently (ESE) before zigzagging steeply up to a tall cairn and felled *Monumento Natural* post (W.11 185M) overlooking the welcome sight of **Playa de la Guancha**. Don't get too excited, though. The descent takes longer than it looks. Winding steeply down the far side of the ridge, we pass a rough bar-gate and metal posts that once carried a chain handrail, after which we descend steadily to the stream bed (Wp.12 195M). Crossing the stream bed, we follow a clear path along its left bank before rejoining the watercourse and eventually passing between a couple of stone beach huts, emerging on the beach between a white cabin and rubber life buoy (Wp.13 210M). By this time, a swim will probably seem imperative, but remember, all Gomeran beaches are potentially dangerous and this particular beach shelves very steeply – you are very much on your own here.

Continuing along the pebble-lined path in front of the white cabin, we pass animal pens and chicken coops before bearing left up a minor *barranco*. The *barranco* path runs into a roughly paved trail climbing steadily (NE) up the **Costado de la Guancha** before bearing right on a gentler gradient for a long ESE traverse (visible from the beach). A final steep climb leads to another *Monumento Natural* signpost (Wp.14 230M), after which a broad clear trail running along a contour line gradually brings **San Sebastián** into sight. After dipping down (NW) to cross the **Revolcadero** watercourse (Wp.15 250M), we climb (NE) past a small ruin (Wp.16 260M). The trail then levels out before descending gently to pass a threshing circle (Wp.17 265M), after which it crosses bare rock for its final steady descent (NW) to the town's power plant (Wp.18 275M), where we turn right on the riverbed-track to the promenade.

**Short Version**

To find Wp.18 in reverse, turn inland 75 metres from the southern end of **San Sebastian** promenade, at a blue kiosk above the penultimate, double-staircase to the beach, and take the riverbed-track past the UNELCO power plant. The path, identified by a red-and-white waymark, starts 200 metres from the beach, immediately after the UNELCO gates, on a concrete way running alongside a green fence and green pipe. Once on the path, it's easy to follow, except on the rise above the port. When you see a rough wooden cross to your left, veer right as indicated by a waymark and traverse bare rock, after which the way is obvious.

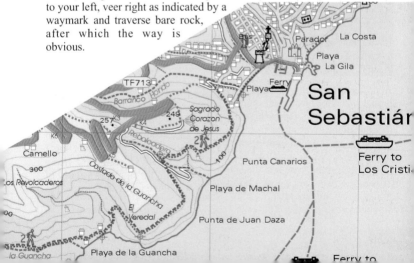

In terms of volcanic history, La Gomera has been a peaceable place for several million years, but the *roques*, bulky little peaks fashioned by erosion round lava fills, are a reminder of less tranquil times. Climbing to the most celebrated cluster of *roques* (**Agando**, **Carmen**, **Zarcita** and **Ojila**), this circuit combines perfectly contrasting ascents and descents, going up through a lugubrious pine forest and coming down across classic Gomeran hillside, all light and expansive views with tiny terraces tucked between converging watersheds. Better still, the route is so beautifully simple, description is virtually, though not quite, superfluous. Parking at **La Laja** isn't easy, but there are a few spaces west of the starting point, just under 1 km from the **La Laja** village limit sign. There's more room further up the road where it runs into concrete. If joining the walk from the bus-stop at Wp.12, ignore Wps.1-2.

4 | 3H 5M | 10.5 km | 700m / 700m | | 2

**Access**: by car and (from Wp.12) bus 🚌 L1 or L2

**Stroll**: the sharp rocks east of the *área recreativa* are a good natural *mirador*.
**Extension**: taxi to La Laja and descend to San Sebastian via Walk 1 or 2

Our walk starts midway through the straggly settlement of **La Laja**, opposite a transformer tower with a park authority signboard for 'Roque Agando 3' (Wp.1 0M). Taking the path descending from the road (S), we turn sharp right after 15 metres and cross a concrete footbridge 50 metres upstream.

The upper houses of La Laja

Climbing steeply up a small spur, we pass behind house No.26 and in front of No.29. Bearing left away from No.32 and right below the next, unnumbered house, we come to a pillar signpost indicating 'Degollada de Peraza' to the left and 'Roque Agando' to the right (Wp.2 10M). Turning right, we pass the last houses of **La Laja**, one evidently owned by a sculptor with a bleakly comic vision of humanity, after which we come to another pillar signpost (Wp.3 15M) where we fork left and resume our steady climb.

And that's about all you need to know for the ascent. There are no major branch paths and no obscure stretches between here and the top. What follows is simply a means of measuring progress. The path bears away from **La Laja** into one of the many affluents feeding the **Barranco de las Lajas**, the flanks of which are studded with a splendid array of house-leeks. Crossing the watercourse (Wp.4 35M), we climb through mixed pine and eucalyptus, traversing a stubby rise into the next *barranco*, which is itself split into two affluents, crossed via wooden bridges (Wps.5 40M & 6 45M). After a third bridge a few minutes later, we climb steadily to a semi-ruinous but superbly situated forestry worker's hut (Wp.7 60M) from where we have fine views of

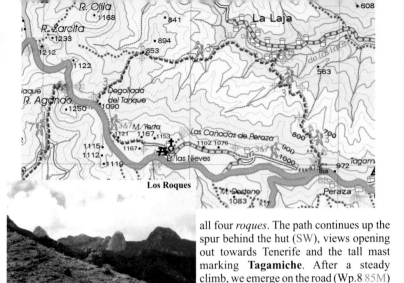

all four *roques*. The path continues up the spur behind the hut (SW), views opening out towards Tenerife and the tall mast marking **Tagamiche**. After a steady climb, we emerge on the road (Wp.8 85M) just east of **Roque Agando**.

Turning left, we follow the road for 200 metres and, at the end of the crash barriers, bear left on a cobbled path that climbs steadily to a narrow cutting, beyond which we join the end of an old dirt track (Wp.9 100M) leading to the barbecue sheds and picnic tables at the **Ermita de las Nieves** *área recreativa* (Wp.10 105M). We continue along the tarmac access road to the east and, shortly before it swings sharp right to descend to the main road, bear left on a stony track marked with a cairn (Wp.11 115M). Ignoring two branches on the left, we follow this track across a barren *lomo* with fine views of Tenerife and the south-eastern *barrancos*. The track eventually runs into a roughly cobbled path that ends in a mildly vertiginous descent to the road, west of the **Playa de Santiago** turn-off. Just east of the junction, is the **Degollada de Peraza** bus-stop and *mirador* (Wp.12 130M), the starting point for those without a car.

Our descent to **La Laja** starts immediately next to the bus-stop. Like the ascent, once you're on it, there's no going wrong. All you have to do is stick to the main cobbled trail and ignore all branch paths. Whereas our ascent was, for the most part, crowded into narrow ravines flanked by trees, the descent cuts across open land speckled with palm trees and agave, with consistently good views across the **Barranco de las Lajas**.

Winding down along the cobbled donkey trail, we pass a small ruin (Wp.13 145M) and a pillar signpost (Wp.14 150M). After several glimpses of individual clusters of houses in **La Laja**, we round a corner onto a level stretch of trail (Wp.15 160M) from where we have clear views of the entire settlement and, up the valley, of the *roques*.

At the end of the level stretch, a series of tight zigzags descend to cross the watercourse of a narrow *barranco* (Wp.16 170M), after which we climb over a small rise for our final, picture-postcard descent to **La Laja**. Rejoining our outward route at the **Roque Agando** pillar signpost (Wp.2 180M), motorists turn right and those who arrived by bus, bear left to pick up the walk as described above.

# 4. PISTA FORESTAL DE MAJONA & PLAYA DE LA CALETA

This lengthy but easy traverse is ideal for inexperienced walkers wanting to try a long distance hike through remote terrain without any pathfinding problems. Which is not to say more experienced walkers won't enjoy it. The views are great and it's a good introduction to the *barranco* architecture of La Gomera, but since most of the itinerary (all if preferred) is on well-stabilised dirt track, the walking itself is not particularly challenging - just a matter of one step after another and considerable stamina!

*includes La Caleta

**Access**: by bus 🚌 L3 or L5. Ask for the **Pista** or **Camino Forestal de Majona**.
See 'taxis' in Appendix B to avoid walking up the main road at the end.
If arriving by car to do Short Version (a), the track is 5.7 km from **San Sebastian** city limits.

**Short Versions**
**(a)** turn right at Wp.6 and follow the track back to the start
**(b)** & **(c)** to **Playa de la Caleta** from **Hermigua**, either as a linear walk descending directly from Wp.19, or climbing the dirt track to Wp.13 to do the **El Palmar** loop.

From the junction with the TF713 (Wp.1 0M), we set off on the **Majona** *pista forestal* and, 30 metres after the start of the patterned concrete surfacing, branch left on a cobbled path marked with a green arrow and *Parque Natural* signpost; alternatively, for a longer but less steep start, stay on the track, rejoining the described itinerary at Wp.6.

The path climbs alongside a dry watercourse before veering right (E), curving round a large outcrop of rock on a spur, bringing into view a rock 'bridge' high above us on the **Altos de Utera** ridge. After climbing along the eastern side of the spur, we zigzag onto its back behind the outcrop of rock (Wp.2 15M). Still favouring the eastern flank of the spur, the path levels out for 100 metres, after which zigzags lead us across a watershed before returning to the spur, bringing **Roque Agando** into view (Wp.3 30M). We then wind up onto a narrow pine fringed pass (Wp.4 35M), 150 metres west of the 'bridge', at which point we can see Tenerife, the *pista forestal*, and the first of the three ravines crossed on this itinerary, **Barranco de Palopique**.

Turning left, we follow a good dirt path along the northern side of the **Utera** ridge, passing the first of the red-and-white waymarks that accompany us for the remainder of our route. The path runs parallel to the *pista forestal*, cutting through a rock pass on a spur (Wp.5 45M) from where we see **Enchereda** farm, famed for its goat cheese, though the only livestock I saw were a handful of disconsolate looking pigs! A gentle, slightly overgrown descent brings us back to the dirt track (Wp.6 55M), where we again bear left. We follow this track for nearly two hours until the junction at Wp.13. There is no risk of straying off trail, so the following notes are merely for timekeeping.

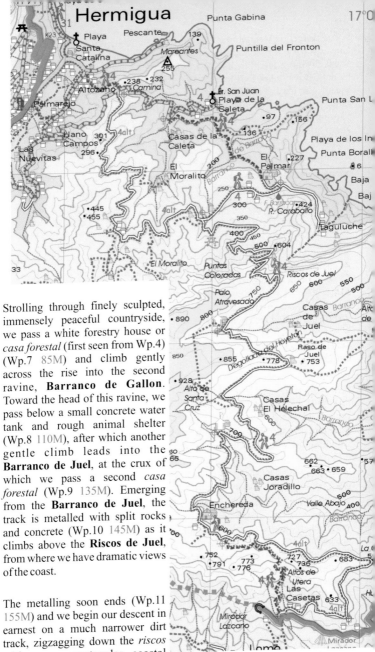

Strolling through finely sculpted, immensely peaceful countryside, we pass a white forestry house or *casa forestal* (first seen from Wp.4) (Wp.7 85M) and climb gently across the rise into the second ravine, **Barranco de Gallon**. Toward the head of this ravine, we pass below a small concrete water tank and rough animal shelter (Wp.8 110M), after which another gentle climb leads into the **Barranco de Juel**, at the crux of which we pass a second *casa forestal* (Wp.9 135M). Emerging from the **Barranco de Juel**, the track is metalled with split rocks and concrete (Wp.10 145M) as it climbs above the **Riscos de Juel**, from where we have dramatic views of the coast.

The metalling soon ends (Wp.11 155M) and we begin our descent in earnest on a much narrower dirt track, zigzagging down the *riscos* with more spectacular coastal views. After passing a concrete bend (Wp.12 160M), the zigzags become so tight they almost touch save for the 50 metre drops in between. We then pass a small abandoned cabin, the only shelter on this route, after which longer, gentler descents, first west, then north-east, then west, bring us down past a small spring/picnic area to the junction with the main **Hermigua-Taguluche** dirt track (Wp.13 190M).

If you're feeling weary, turn left here and follow the dirt track to the tarmac lane at Wp.19. If motivated by powerful thirst, keen hunger, a strong wish to swim, or simply an invincible desire always to do more, turn right as indicated by the GR waymark for **Playa de la Caleta** – an extra 200-metre descent and <u>ascent</u>. The track passes between the rusting remains of a Morris Minor and a rapidly declining farmhouse, after which we pass three more houses of varying size and health. 150 metres after '**Fuente de la Berraca**', we turn sharp left between red posts (Wp.14 210M) and descend to the scruffy, but tremendously friendly **El Palmar** farm, where the dirt track ends (Wp.15 215M) at a rock with 'La Caleta' painted on it.

The beach, seen from the second 'horn'.

From the farm, a faint path, initially running alongside a green fence and dotted with cairns throughout, winds down through rocks to cross a footbridge in the **Barranco de la Barraca** (Wp.16 225M). A clear, slightly vertiginous path, then crosses two 'horns' at the tip of a ridge, from the second of which we can see the beach.

Steps descend from the second horn onto a broad but still intermittently vertiginous path up the **Caleta** valley, which we eventually cross behind cultivated terraces before climbing onto a tarmac lane (Wp.17 245M) 10M from the beach. En route to the beach, we pass the first of two shortcut paths, this one following a narrow eroded ridge.

Swimming is safe at **La Caleta** <u>when the sea is calm</u>. Antonio's restaurant, which he says is open all year (Tel. 667-954-907 to check), serves the usual Canarian specialities and good fresh fish (*pescado fresco* – ask to see it: even if you speak Spanish you probably won't know the local name). If lunch proves altogether too good, Antonio can call a taxi, otherwise we have a long slog up the new tarmac lane.

The first shortcut serves no great purpose, but the second (Wp.18 280M) is useful, rejoining the lane (Wp.19 285M) just below the junction with the **Taguluche** track. Crossing the lane, we take a clear, cairn-marked path winding down an exposed spur. After passing a small empty house and an older ruin, we descend behind the northernmost inhabited houses of **Altozano** onto a concrete path leading to the road (Wp.20 300M).

**Note:**
If doing this in reverse, the path starts next to signposts for 'Playa de la Caleta' and 'Piscinas Naturales de Pescante'. Leave the concrete path before it reaches the first house, bearing left on a dirt path marked with a cairn.

Crossing the bridge over the **Monteforte** watercourse, we pass **Pizzeria Los Prismas** and **Bar/Restaurante El Faro** before climbing to the main road (Wp.21 315M).

**See the notes on GPS use and waypoints on page 18.**

**1.**
**DEGOLLADA DE PERAZA - SAN SEBASTIÁN**

| Wp | N | W |
|---|---|---|
| 1 | 28 05.9754 | 17 11.0802 |
| 2 | 28 05.9124 | 17 10.8210 |
| 3 | 28 05.9538 | 17 10.6116 |
| 4 | 28 06.1524 | 17 10.3800 |
| 5 | 28 06.1350 | 17 10.2516 |
| 6 | 28 06.0372 | 17 09.9738 |
| 7 | 28 05.9952 | 17 09.7752 |
| 8 | 28 05.8470 | 17 09.3048 |
| 9 | 28 05.7360 | 17 08.8272 |
| 10 | 28 05.7222 | 17 08.5374 |
| 11 | 28 05.6760 | 17 08.1504 |
| 12 | 28 05.6286 | 17 07.9632 |
| 13 | 28 05.5830 | 17 07.7184 |
| 14 | 28 05.4666 | 17 07.3086 |
| 15 | 28 05.4480 | 17 06.8628 |

**2.**
**ROQUE SOMBRERO & PLAYA DE LA GUANCHA**

| Wp | N | W |
|---|---|---|
| 1 | 28 05.7714 | 17 09.6324 |
| 2 | 28 05.7630 | 17 09.8790 |
| 3 | 28 05.3994 | 17 09.7398 |
| 4 | 28 05.2236 | 17 09.5832 |
| 5 | 28 05.1666 | 17 09.5646 |
| 6 | 28 05.0280 | 17 09.4170 |
| 7 | 28 04.8390 | 17 09.2412 |
| 8 | 28 04.8162 | 17 09.0924 |
| 9 | 28 04.6038 | 17 09.2022 |
| 10 | 28 04.4016 | 17 08.9940 |
| 11 | 28 04.3416 | 17 08.6730 |
| 12 | 28 04.3260 | 17 08.4630 |
| 13 | 28 04.4244 | 17 07.7514 |
| 14 | 28 04.4364 | 17 07.4718 |
| 15 | 28 04.8468 | 17 07.3134 |
| 16 | 28 04.8960 | 17 07.0806 |
| 17 | 28 04.9926 | 17 06.8880 |
| 18 | 28 05.2746 | 17 06.9606 |

**3.**
**LOS ROQUES**

| Wp | N | W |
|---|---|---|
| 1 | 28 06.6648 | 17 11.3466 |
| 2 | 28 06.5766 | 17 11.4468 |
| 3 | 28 06.6606 | 17 11.6256 |
| 4 | 28 06.6048 | 17 11.8932 |
| 5 | 28 06.5868 | 17 11.9730 |
| 6 | 28 06.5832 | 17 12.0804 |
| 7 | 28 06.6402 | 17 12.3138 |
| 8 | 28 06.3480 | 17 12.6474 |
| 9 | 28 06.1380 | 17 12.3240 |
| 10 | 28 06.0894 | 17 12.1602 |
| 11 | 28 06.0552 | 17 11.6814 |
| 12 | 28 05.9862 | 17 11.0790 |
| 13 | 28 06.1824 | 17 11.1798 |
| 14 | 28 06.2664 | 17 11.2260 |
| 15 | 28 06.4254 | 17 11.2452 |
| 16 | 28 06.4770 | 17 11.3892 |

**4.**
**PISTA FORESTAL DE MAJONA & PLAYA DE LA CALETA**

| Wp | N | W |
|---|---|---|
| 1 | 28 07.4226 | 17 09.5160 |
| 2 | 28 07.5624 | 17 09.5466 |
| 3 | 28 07.7028 | 17 09.5550 |
| 4 | 28 07.7526 | 17 09.5202 |
| 5 | 28 07.8480 | 17 09.6972 |
| 6 | 28 07.8816 | 17 09.9006 |
| 7 | 28 08.4972 | 17 09.9384 |
| 8 | 28 08.7096 | 17 09.9102 |
| 9 | 28 09.0804 | 17 09.9090 |
| 10 | 28 09.3306 | 17 09.5580 |
| 11 | 28 09.4104 | 17 09.7536 |
| 12 | 28 09.4758 | 17 09.6198 |
| 13 | 28 09.7356 | 17 10.0986 |
| 14 | 28 09.9000 | 17 09.5058 |
| 15 | 28 09.9480 | 17 09.6594 |
| 16 | 28 10.0680 | 17 09.8778 |
| 17 | 28 10.3128 | 17 10.2996 |
| 18 | 28 10.4664 | 17 10.5846 |
| 19 | 28 10.4958 | 17 10.6482 |
| 20 | 28 10.5918 | 17 10.8678 |
| 21 | 28 10.4640 | 17 11.2200 |

After zig-zagging up from **San Sebastián**, your first view of the south is likely to stay with you forever. Great ravines (*barrancos*) seperated by broad backed ridges (*lomos*) sweep imperiously down to the ocean. The scale of this 'barranco architecture' quite takes your breath away. Impressive steps of abandoned terraces show that this region was once intensively farmed, but now this is just a distant memory. Take a break at **Bar Peraza**, or the **Peraza** *mirador*, to take in the scale of the land and then head down the new road to **Playa Santiago**. Modern tarmac contrasts with small settlements and sun bleached landscapes until we meet the modern south at the Don Tomás development. This is Fred Olsen country, modern villas overlooking a new golf course before dropping down to pass the impressive **Jardin Tecina** hotel; try the lift if you get the chance.

A new road and tunnel diverts traffic away from the town and beach. Once a busy fishing port, until they sold the fishing boats, the small town has settled into a sleepy relaxation while preparing itself for the weekend bar hoping along the seafront. Modern tourism, in the form of the **Jardin Tecina** hotel and **Balcón de Santa Ana** (HPB), now brackets the traditional hostals and the apartment accommodation of **Playa Santiago** and **Laguna de Santiago**.

Inland, the mighty **Benchijigua** and **Guarimar** *barrancos* are home to some of La Gomera's most impressive walking routes, the picturesque settlements a direct contrast to the modern coastal development.

Climbing past **La Trinchera** we pass under the shadow of the new, but little used, airport to zig-zag up to the regional capital of **Alajeró**. Once suffering near terminal depopulation, now returning emigrés are building new villas leading to the town's regeneration, three good bar/restaurants indicating its new found affluence. A stroll south to the **Ermita de San Isidor** on **Calvario** is a must to gaze out over the dramatic landscape that was once back-breakingly farmed. Sleepy, or fast asleep, most of the year, the town is transformed by the Fiesta de Buen Paso, renowned as La Gomera's noisiest fiesta.

Almost opposite the turning to the cliff-side village of **Imada** is the **Drago**, La Gomera's only wild 'Dragon' tree, an easy stroll from the road, or take Walk 11 for a more exciting approach. Once left to its own devices, the **Drago** is now fiercely fenced against souvenir hunters, and has its own manicured path and parking area. The sleepy hamlet of **Igualero**, nestling below the **Garajonay** peak, completes the southern landscapes with a spectacular *mirador* view from its *ermita*.

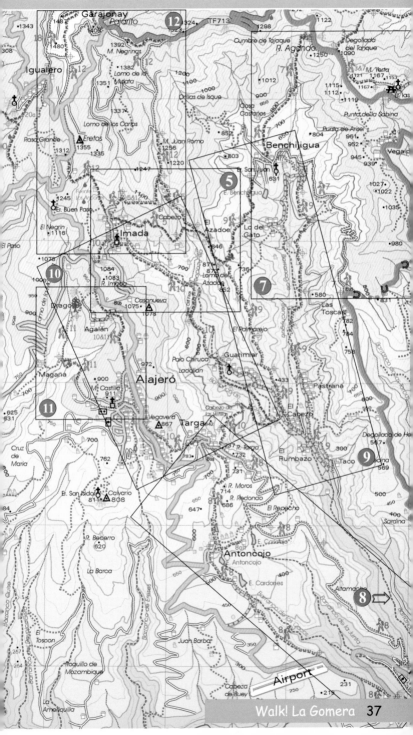

A short walk for those who want to explore this wild corner of the island without any huge climbs or alarming cliff face paths. The **Lomo de Azadoe** pass is included as a link to walks in the **Barranco de Benchijigua**.

| 3 | 1½ H | 4 km | 250m / 250m | | 2 |

**Access**: by car or bus. Parking is limited, but there's usually room in front of the **Bar Arcilia** or at the end of the road.

**Stroll:** to WP3
**Extension**: see Walks 7/9/12

Bus L2 or L6. If arriving by bus L2, add 4 km return for the descent from the **Imada** turn-off. If arriving by bus L6, ask to be dropped off at the **Carretera de Almacigos** and use the path described in Walk 10 Wps.21-20.

Starting in front of the **Bar-Cafeteria Arcilia** (Wp.1 0M), we take the path, marked with a red dot on a white wall, behind the **Colegio Imada** and telephone booth. Turning left at a T-junction after 40 metres, we join a cobbled path leading out of the village. Descending towards palms and ignoring a branch to the right, we stay on the main paved path, crossing the reddish rocks of an affluent to the **Azadoe**.

A dirt, terrace path leads us to steps, some carved directly into the rock, climbing behind a small house to pass in front of a flat-roofed bungalow (Wp.2 10M), from where we have our first excellent views down the **Barrancos de Guarimar** and **Santiago** to **Jardin Tecina**. Sticking to the broader, higher traces, we follow the path round the nose of a spur, passing

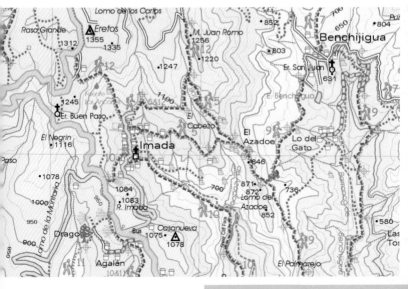

**Fine views of the barrancos**

above an abandoned house and older ruins, onto a small platform from where we see both the **Barranco** and **Lomo de Azadoe** (Wp.3 20M). We then wind down, crossing the *barranco* onto an initially level path that soon climbs above a terrace to a Y-junction (Wp.4 30M).

**To link up with Walks 7 & 9**

We stay on the main right hand branch, passing several ruins before crossing the **Lomo de Azadoe** pass (Wp.5 35M), 100 metres above Wp.8 of Walk 9.

**For a short circular walk**

We bear left at the Y-junction, climbing to two ruins, where the path swings left on a broader, rockier way. The climb, steady at first, gradually becomes gentler then levels off altogether, as we go deeper into the palm fringed ravine, soon glimpsing a small stand of pine; way above us but only a little way above the point we're climbing to! Climbing again, we pass through a riotous mix of prickly pear, agave, wax-plants, house-leeks, bracken, almonds, palms and figs, with the odd vine threaded in between them.

The path levels off again briefly, running below a high retaining wall, before climbing gently and veering right (Wp.6 45M not counting Wp.5) in front of a fig tree, bearing away from the watercourse briefly before coming back to run alongside it for a steadier, partially paved climb. We then veer right again, passing a 'Paisaje Protegido Orone' signpost peppered with gunshot (Wp.7 50M). Climbing south-east, we have more good views of the *barrancos* below us, before resuming our north-westerly ascent. Climbing between terraces, we return to the watercourse above a dry waterfall (Wp.8 65M), joining the route of Walk 12 at Wp.4.

Walk 12 continues up the watercourse, but we turn left, crossing the watercourse to follow the start of Walk 12 back to the village. Heading south-south west (SSW) and passing one very slightly vertiginous stretch above the falls, we round a small spur and see **Imada**. A straightforward descent on an intermittently paved and stepped trail brings us back across the affluent crossed at the start of the walk, this time below an attractive waterfall. We then join the end of the village access road, which we follow back to our starting point.

A dramatic ravine, remote countryside accessible only on foot, and a pristine pebble beach, make this essential walking for anyone wanting to get to know La Gomera. Not recommended in hot weather. If staying in **San Sebastián** or **Valle Gran Rey**, this is a good walk to combine with a return trip on the **Garajonay Exprés** ferry.

| 5 | 3½ H | 14 km | 250m / 1150m | 3 |
|---|---|---|---|---|

**Access**: by bus 🚌 L2 or L5

**Short Version**
**Tecina – Playa del Medio**

🛥️ To return to San Sebastián or Valle Gran Rey

Our walk starts 400 metres (direction, **San Sebastián**) east of **Jerdune** bus-stop on a dirt track (Wp.1 5M) feeding into a bend of the old road, where a 'Monumento Natural Barranco del Cabrito' signpost marks the start of the path along the **Tacalcuse** ridge - for simplicity's sake, I call it a path, though it often widens to a donkey trail. Descending along the western flank of the ridge with fine views over the **Barranco de Chinguarime**, we cross a grassy pass (Wp.2 20M) above a ruined hamlet, after which tiny terraces and cabins perched in improbable crevices on the far side of the ravine attest to the historical poverty of La Gomera –you really had to be desperate to shore up land in some of these places. Staying west of the ridge and ignoring a very faint path branching right, we descend along the main trail below the cliffs of **Alto de Tacalcuse**.

The ruined hamlet.

Approaching the **Alto de Tacalcuse**, the path seems to disappear above crags riddled with half caves. In fact, it narrows to enter the first of three brief but steep climbs (Wp.3 40M) linked by a broad slightly vertiginous ledge below cliffs so roughly fragmented they resemble dry-stone walling. After the third climb, we see the golf-course/hotel complex above **Playa Santiago** and the cliffs behind **Llano de la Cruz**. Continuing in an easterly direction, we cross a broad sloping sheet of rock with steps carved into its lower end, after which we wind between boulders, passing a cabin built into the overhanging cliffs (Wp.4 55M). We then climb across terraces to a Y-junction (Wp.5 65M). The broader trail continues (SE) to **El Cabrito**, but we turn right (S) to cross **Llano de la Cruz** on a minor, but clear and level path flanked by terrace walls.

After passing between a buried reservoir and two natural watering holes, we descend across a wide, open sweep of terraces. Ignoring minor dirt paths along the terraces, we stick to the main rocky trail defined by crumbling walls, passing to the right of two ruins (Wp.6 75M), invisible from above but the first of many on this route. The path gets clearer, descending between two more

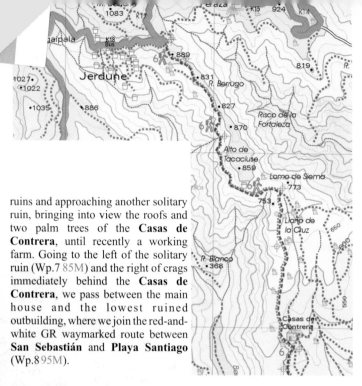

ruins and approaching another solitary ruin, bringing into view the roofs and two palm trees of the **Casas de Contrera**, until recently a working farm. Going to the left of the solitary ruin (Wp.7 85M) and the right of crags immediately behind the **Casas de Contrera**, we pass between the main house and the lowest ruined outbuilding, where we join the red-and-white GR waymarked route between **San Sebastián** and **Playa Santiago** (Wp.8 95M).

Turning right, we descend a narrow, winding path, crossing (Wp.9 100M) then re-crossing one of the watercourses that subsequently carve out the **Barranco de la Vasa**. After following the watercourse for a while, we climb a small rise, where we ignore a branch path to a cluster of houses on the eastern side of the main watercourse. Sticking to the main path, which is boundary-marked with splashes of green paint, we descend past two small farm buildings (one apparently still maintained), passing occult (both in intent and the very approximate grasp of Spanish grammar) graffiti babbling about weird goings-on under the full moon. 100 metres later, we re-cross the watercourse (Wp.10 110M) and follow its right bank as it broadens and deepens into **Barranco de la Vasa**. After the next ruin, the path briefly disappears, but maintaining direction (S) across a slab of bare rock, we soon recover it, passing two more ruins before running alongside (and briefly in) a shallow watershed. Passing one more ruin, we bear south-west, traversing the brow of a hill, after which we have a gentle then steady descent into the **Barranco de Chinguarime** (Wp.11 145M), where we cross the riverbed and join a dirt track.

50 metres after a breeze block water hut, we branch right on a waymarked path (Wp.12 150M), every bit as strenuous as it looks from the far side, climbing to pass in front of the lowest **Joradillo** farm-building, where we bear right on a clear path descending into the **Barranco Biquillo**. Rejoining the dirt track (Wp.13 170M) in the *barranco*, it's a question of different strokes for different folks: those who will do anything for a dip, bear left for **Playa del Medio**; those for whom the very thought of swimming at this stage of a walk is enough to have them swooning into their rucksacks, bear right.

**If you descend to the beach** (safe swimming when calm)
- look for a GR-waymark just west of the parking area (Wp.14 175M) indicating a way back to the dirt track via abandoned terraces. There's no single path, just a series of beaten ways, constantly diverging and converging, but all aiming for the dentated crash barriers on the ridge, where a blue hieroglyph and red arrow lead us onto a bend of the dirt track, 50 metres along which we turn left on a path descending into the **Barranco de Tapahuga**.

**If you take the non-swimming option**
- turn sharp right just before the cusp of the dirt track on a path doubling back towards the **Villa Maria**. When you see a GR waymark, step over the canal onto a path that re-crosses the dirt track on the far side of the ridge and descends into the **Barranco de Tapahuga**.

The final stretch is being redeveloped. At present, **Playa de Tapahuga** is accessed by a dirt track, but it seems likely a new road from **Hotel Jardin Tecina** will extend all the way into this *barranco*. Happily the route is straightforward, so whatever changes are made, they won't cause any pathfinding problems. Climbing up the track/road, we come to a Y-junction (Wp.15 195M); the right hand branch will certainly be asphalted, the left hand branch maybe. The new road to the right is more direct, but the traditional route forks left. This track/lane runs between abandoned banana plantations to the Olsen banana warehouse, where we turn right on a tarmac lane climbing to rejoin the new road just east of the **Hotel Jardin Tecina**. Turning left, we stroll past the hotel to the main road (Wp.16 210M), where there's a phone booth, taxi stand, bus-stop and the **Restaurante Tagoror**.

**If you want to descend to the seafront**, take the stepped shortcut starting just left of the **Restaurante Tagoror**.

If you're doing the **Short Version**, the lane down to the warehouse is the first open turning after the **Hotel Jardin Tecina**.

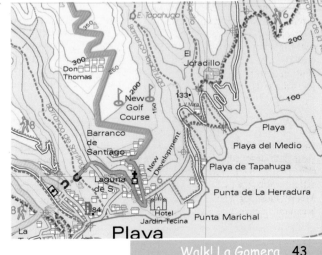

# 7. LAS TOSCAS - DEGOLLADA DE PERAZA

Like a tour of the entire island in miniature, this walk encompasses the four key features that characterise the La Gomeran landscape: a *barranco*, a hamlet, a *roque* and an *ermita*. It's also a useful linking route for piecing together longer itineraries.

| 4 | 2¾ H | 10 km | 600m / 300m | ⟷ | 2 |

**Access**: by bus 🚌 L2 or L5 to **Las Toscas**, L1 or L2 or L5 from **Peraza**

**Short Version**
Benchijigua – Roque Agando

**Extension**s: see Walks 1/2/9

From **Las Toscas**, we take the *pista forestal* for 'Benchijigua/Lo del Gato' (Wp.1 0M), a driveable dirt track, but sufficiently dramatic to be worth walking. After a long steady descent with constantly unfolding views over the **Barranco de Benchijigua**, we pass the tarmac lane down to **Lo del Gato** (Wp.2 45M).

Continuing on the dirt track through **Benchijigua**, we bear right at a Y-junction, 150 metres after which we turn sharp right for 'Agando' on a minor track behind a long low yellow building identifiable by a ceramic 'Benchijigua' nameplate (Wp.3 55M).

A rain-drenched Barranco de Benchijigua

When the track splits in three, we take the right-hand branch, a broad walking trail that swings east after 75 metres, climbing past a small ruin concealing a couple of water tanks. The trail becomes increasingly rocky as it winds up a wide ridge behind the ruin, rapidly gaining height before skirting to the right of a small, roughly conical peak and heading towards the distinctive bulk of **Roque Agando** (NE). After a steady climb, the trail levels out amid immense agave-scapes before dipping slightly and narrowing to a path as it approaches then climbs to cross the **Canal de Benchijigua** (Wp.4 85M).

After the canal, a clear but narrow path climbs to the left of **Roque Agando**, passing through dense, remarkably varied vegetation. The path gradually broadens, crossing intermittent paving and stone steps, as scruffy heath trees gradually replace the more varied flora. It then levels out very briefly,

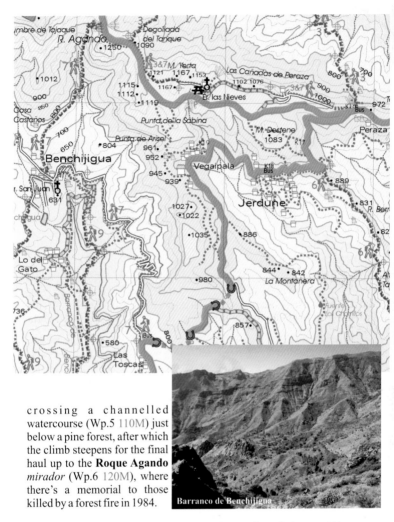

crossing a channelled watercourse (Wp.5 110M) just below a pine forest, after which the climb steepens for the final haul up to the **Roque Agando** *mirador* (Wp.6 120M), where there's a memorial to those killed by a forest fire in 1984.

Barranco de Benchijigua

Bearing right, we follow the road east, joining Walk 3 a little over 100 metres later at a sign for 'La Laja'. We follow Walk 3, Wps. 8-12 to the **Degollada de Peraza** bus-stop, beyond which there's a simple bar/restaurant.

# 8. PLAYA SANTIAGO - TARGA

If you're looking for pristine nature, either skip this one altogether or restrict yourself to Short Version (b). The land adjacent to **Playa Santiago** and the airport is badly degraded and can only disappoint anyone hoping to experience something lush and unspoiled. If, on the other hand, you want a big, uncomplicated climb with good views and a little off-path adventure half way round, then this circuit has a lot to recommend it. Don't even think about it in hot weather though – the word 'toast' comes to mind.

*+ 40M return for the extension
**3 in Playa Santiago, 4 including the extension

**Short Versions**
**(a)** bus to the **Targa** turn-off and do the descent
**(b)** If you don't fancy a big climb but want to see the **Barranco de los Cocos**, bus/drive to **Antoncojo** and follow the access road to the turning circle at its end (motorists park here). A concrete ramp descends from the turning circle to a faint path that crosses terraces and climbs a small rise before ending at a solitary house. Bearing left (N) we pick up faint traces of goat paths, which we follow (NE) to the head of the **Barranco de la Junta**. Goats are chronic nonconformists and there's no such thing as a single path here, only a series of meandering ways, but it's easy walking and all we have to do is aim midway between a large farmhouse and tumbledown cane shelter on the far side of the *barranco*, where an old but clear trail climbs to join the main itinerary below Wp.6.

**Stroll**:
**La Trinchera – Playa Santiago**

**Extension**: **Restaurante Palmeras** (see text)***

**Access** by car and 🚌 bus L2 or L5

From **Playa Santiago** seafront, we cross the square between **Caja Canarias** bank and **Bodegon del Mar** (Wp.1 0M), and take a back street to the 'Centro Salud', where we turn left into the dry riverbed. Following the riverbed dirt track, we go under a bridge and pass the high school before branching right, climbing to cross the **Alajero** road. Just before the 'Aeropuerto 3' sign (Wp.2 15M), we take a rock strewn track, the old 'road', which we follow all the way to **Targa**. There are numerous shortcuts en route, but they're all rough and obscure, so I suggest sticking to the main track. Otherwise the ascent is straightforward and all you really need to know is that the tall red-and-white mast seen on the horizon after twenty-five minutes of climbing, is our objective.

The track climbs past a water tank tucked in a quarry, then winds up the ridge dividing the **Barrancos de la Junta** and **Santiago**, to a point dominating both sides of **Playa Santiago** (Wp.3 35M). The views improve steadily as we climb past a path leading to a ruin on our right (Wp.4 60M), at which point we can see **Antoncojo** (our return route) to the north-west. We then pass the gate-posted entrance to a second ruin and climb to a large dry reservoir (Wp.5 80M), after which the track bears west towards **Antoncojo**, passing below an abandoned cabin. Ignoring two tracks and a donkey trail branching left, we approach the head of the **Barranco de la Junta**, shortly before which, our track swings sharp right (E), climbing to pass below a more substantial ruin (Wp.6 100M). The track gets grassier on the last stretch of the climb, finally passing the first of several half built houses and the red-and-white mast (Wp.7 130M), 150 metres after which we reach the tarmac lane through **Targa**.

Our descent begins 200 metres along this lane, just past a dull orange house with decorative stones set in its walls (Wp.8 140M). However, if you want food and can face a further 50 metres climbing, you may wish to consider the extension.

**\*\*Extension**
Continuing past the orange house, we turn left onto the main horseshoe lane through **Targa**. We leave this lane 50 metres later, immediately after a small bridge, turning right between the bridge and a single storey building with large green garage doors. We then bear left up a rocky slope to join a path climbing towards the large yellow reservoir visible above. Rejoining the horseshoe lane just below the reservoir, we turn left and, 50 metres later, immediately after an old quarry blocked with boulders, right on a broad donkey trail. Turning right at a T-junction and crossing a broad shelf of rock, we join the path that emerges in front of the **Las Palmeras Restaurant**.

**Descent from Targa**
Just north of the orange house, we turn left if ascending, right if descending from the extension or doing Short Version (a), on a broad trail marked with a cairn and red dot. After crossing large slabs of exposed rock, the trail dwindles to a narrow path running between old terracing walls and following a thin metal pipe. The path passes below a new breeze block bungalow, bearing right, away from the pipe, and winding down over more exposed rock before roughly paved zigzags bring us down to the **Barranco de los Cocos** watercourse (Wp.9 155M excluding the extension), where we begin a virtually pathless descent to **Antoncojo**.

Crossing sloping rocks on the left bank, we descend into the watercourse itself below a wall flanking an old reservoir, after which another faint 'path', again on the left bank, descends toward a palm grove in small terraced fields, where we have to squeeze past an overhanging rock. Another short stretch in the bed of the *barranco* is followed by a third left-bank 'path', where we briefly glimpse **Antoncojo**. We then drop back into the watercourse for 150 metres. Winding between rock pools and picking our way through the rocks (<u>very</u> gingerly if they happen to be wet), we look for a faint 'path' on the right bank (Wp.10 170M) leading to tiny crumbling terraces. These are fairly easily identified as they are backed by a concrete covered canal curving smoothly along the right stroke of the ravine's V-shaped horizon. If you happen to miss the first branch of this 'path' and find yourself above a small waterfall overlooking a mini-reservoir, backtrack 30 metres to find a cairn-marked access onto the terraces. Following a very faint way, we climb across the terraces, aiming for the point where the canal descends from a low orange

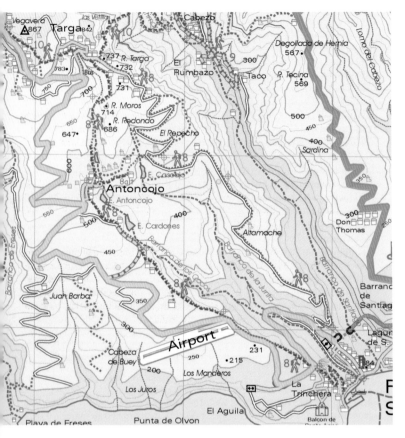

crag, where we join a reasonably clear path next to a concrete nameplate commemorating 'Francisco Diaz Barroso' (Wp.11 175M).

Antoncojo

We follow this path past a more substantial dam into **Antoncojo**. Sticking to the same path through the village, we join the end of a tarmac road leading to a T-junction. Turning right at the T-junction, we follow the road for 75 metres, taking the second metalled (a dirt track at the time of writing, but I'm assured it will be asphalted!) branch on the left (S) (Wp.12 185M).

200 metres along this track/lane, just before it climbs back toward the road, we turn left (SE) on a clear donkey trail that has recently been re-paved for the first few metres. The trail, which soon runs into older, rougher paving, follows

two pipes, one clad in stone, the other exposed with 'Buderus' stencilled on its side. The trail disappears in a new tarmac lane next to a house with sunflowers painted on its wall. We follow the lane for 100 metres, passing the **Embalse Cardones** dam wall, 100 metres after which the lane bears right (SW) and we carry straight on (SE) (Wp.13 200M) crossing the stone-clad water pipe and recovering the old trail.

We descend along the pipe-path behind two small farmhouses, the first with some surprising livestock, after which the 'Buderus' pipe resurfaces. Ignoring all paintmarks and cairns marking apparent ways back into the **Barranco de los Cocos** (they don't, or at least nothing you'd care to take without feathers or cloven hooves) we follow the pipes to the road (Wp.14 220M) above the airport. Continuing on the road for 600 metres, we pass the airport entrance, 100 metres after which, immediately before the start of green fencing on the left, we slip through the crash barriers to recover the pipe-path, which runs into dirt track just above **La Trinchera**.

Maintaining direction (SE) we descend to a dangerous bend in the road (Wp.15 235M), which we cross <u>very</u> quickly (think 'Roadrunner') onto a concrete and stone path leading to a *mirador* overlooking **Playa Santiago**. Continuing along the lane behind the *mirador*, we turn left at a 'retevision' transmitter. Concrete steps lead to a spectacular path, snaking its way down to join our outward route 200 metres from the seafront.

# 9. BARRANCO DE BENCHIJIGUA

This is one of the classics: hidden idyllic hamlets, gullies quilted with smallholdings, crumbling ruins conjuring DIY dreams, and a landscape that, despite its low altitude, has a real 'high mountain' feel to it. To reach the start, take the **Taco/Guarimiar** road behind **Playa Santiago**. The walk starts at the **Taco/Pastrana** Y-junction. Park 50 metres up the **Pastrana** road.

| | | | | | |
|---|---|---|---|---|---|
| 5 | 4 H | 12 km | 600m / 600m | ↻ | 0 |

**Access**: by car. Non-motorists taxi to **El Cabezo** and return via the road at the end of the day. The first 2 kilometres are pleasant. Only the last kilometre approaching the main road is disagreeable.

**Short Version**
Bus to **Las Toscas**, follow Walk 7 to **Benchijigua**, then descend as described from Wp.11

**Strolls** (from **Benchijigua**, for motorists)
**(a)** Wps.11-9
**(b)** Wps.11-14 then cross to **Lo del Gato** and return by the road
**(c)** scrambling up to the caves behind **Ermita San Juan**

Branching left at the **Taco/Pastrana** Y-junction (Wp.1 0M), we follow the road through **Taco,** passing turn-offs to **El Rumbazo** (left) and into the **Barranco de Benchijigua** (right), after which we climb steadily for a little under 10 minutes before branching right into the hamlet of **El Cabezo**, perched on the thin ridge of rock at the tip of **Lomo de Azadoe**. Directly behind the first house, **Casa Maria Angeles** (Wp.2 15M), we cross a sheet of rock onto concrete and stone steps.

Ignoring minor branches to the right, we follow a roughly cobbled path climbing along the western flank of the *lomo*, passing to the left of a small water tower and coming into view of the **Ermita de Guarimiar**.

The path winds up to skirt a large outcrop of rock before crossing (roughly parallel with the *ermita*) onto the eastern flank of the *lomo*, bringing us into sight of **Roque Agando** and our return path on the far side of the ravine (Wp.3 45M). Approaching the large 'bowler hat' bluffs defining the heights of the *lomo*, we briefly cross back onto its western flank, before definitively returning to the eastern flank, where we must take care not to lose the cobbled path when it bears right (N) and a dirt path continues directly ahead (W) (Wp.4 55M).

Rounding the bluffs, our path runs into grubby-golden rock (Wp.5 60M) and the 'bowler-hat' reveals itself as something more akin to a crocodile snout. The path occasionally disappears in the rock, but there's only one way for a sane person to go up here, and we soon pick up its traces again. After a steady climb, we traverse a large, stubby spur (Wp.6 70M) jutting out from the *lomo*, immediately after which we cross a flattened fence of orange plastic mesh. Another steady climb brings us across the back of the next spur, 100 metres after which the gradient eases and we fork left at a Y-junction (Wp.7 85M)

We now traverse a hillside dotted with palm and agave, the latter with scapes so tall in soil so dry they frequently topple over. This last stretch of the climb seems to go on interminably, but eventually, after a little over 15 minutes, we cross a slab of reddish, lightly fissured rock onto a level path from where we can see, way below us, the final stretch of our outward route, snaking along to pass behind the long ridge of rock separating **Benchijigua** from **Lo del Gato**. The level path leads to a junction (Wp.8 105M) with a major, waymarked path climbing from the east and leading up to the pass over **Lomo de Azadoe**.

Toppling agaves

Turning right at the junction, we zigzag down the steep slope before a gentler descent leads to a sheet of rock that appears to have been used as a threshing circle, after which we wind round behind a small ruin (Wp.9 130M), an excellent spot for a picnic or to shelter from inclement weather, and worth a visit to see the old bread oven at its south-eastern corner and the traditional cane ceiling inside – mind you, somebody has taken the trouble to daub 'Danger' on the wall, a sufficiently rare concept in S p a i n  t o  b e  w o r t h considering.

From here it's an easy stroll to the junction (Wp.10 140M identified by red and blue waymarks if you're doing this route in reverse) with the d i r t  t r a c k  b e t w e e n Benchijigua and its dam. Turning left, we follow the track as it climbs gently round the head of the valley, coming into the hamlet next to a building with a ceramic 'Benchijigua' nameplate (Wp.11 150M).

The old oven, 130 minutes into the route.

**Note**
If following this route in reverse or doing Stroll (a)., the track is chained and marked by red and blue dots and a wooden signpost for 'Imada'. Ignore a branch left 50 metres after the chain.

75 metres along the main track out of **Benchijigua**, we branch right on a path spotted with enough waymarks to fill a test card. The path passes below one of the *casas rurales* for which the hamlet is famous and crosses a dry watercourse to run along a terrace before descending towards a large ruin where we bear left. Winding round to cross another watercourse, we pass through a long zigzag, crossing yet another watercourse just above the **Lo del Gato** road, which we join 75 metres later at a small culvert (Wp.12 165M). Bearing left, we go up the road 50 metres to a U-bend, just before which a large cairn marks the start of our path, branching off to the right.

Once on this good, broad, partially stepped path, we simply have to follow it all the way to Wp.16, ignoring all branches, so the following is merely for time-keeping. The path climbs a small rise, bringing us into view of the hamlet of **Lo del Gato** and its neatly terraced fields. We then descend steadily to cross a canal, one of the few open canals on the island still with running water (Wp.13 175M), after which we wind down alongside a torrent of boulders before bearing left across the broad pleated slope facing **Lo del Gato**. Ignoring (unless following Stroll (b)) a major branch right to **Lo del Gato** (Wp.14 190M), we carry straight on across rusty coloured rocks mottled with seams of ochre and pale yellow. We also ignore another, minor, cairn-marked branch (Wp.15 200M) doubling back to the right, and continue on the main path toward an electricity pylon, shortly before which we pass a very slightly vertiginous stretch. After a second pylon, we pass between a ruin and two reservoirs and descend into the bed of the *barranco* (Wp.16 215M).

With the help of occasional blue dashes on the rocks, we pick our way through the boulders in the middle of the watercourse to a tiny locked cabin on the right bank, 50 metres downstream. After following a faint path running alongside large brown water pipes on the right bank for another 50 metres, we cross onto a paved trail climbing the left bank. This runs into a path leading up to **Pastrana** and the end of the road (Wp.17 235M) which we follow back to our starting point.

# 10. BARRANCO DE GUARIMIAR

One sometimes has the impression that in the days before TV, game-boys and karaoke, bored but playful Gomerans would studiously pick out apparently impassable cliff faces and make paths up them just to pass the time. To be fair, they didn't have much choice if they wanted to go anywhere, yet you can't help but wonder. In this strenuous circuit, we use two of the most improbable paths you're likely to encounter anywhere, one dropping down (I use the phrase advisedly) from the hamlet of **Targa** into the **Barranco de Guarimiar**, the other climbing the same ravine to **Imada**. Not to be missed, unless you suffer from vertigo.

**Access**: by bus  L2 or L6 or car.

**Restaurante Las Palmeras** is midway between the two **Alajeró** bus-stops.

**Stroll**
Even if you don't do the full walk, it's worth looking at the start of the descent. The cave at Wp.6 is an ideal niche for settling down and drinking in the view.

**Short Version**
Turn right at Wp.14 to follow the track and road to **Playa Santiago**.

From the eastern end of the **Ayuntamiento de Alajeró** car-park (Wp.1 0M), we take a lane on the right down to the principal road through the village, which we follow south, branching left at the Y-junction to join the **Playa Santiago** road. Maintaining direction (S), we descend to the **Bar/Restaurante Las Palmeras**, opposite which we take a broad, newly paved donkey trail (Wp.2 10M). The trail narrows to a dirt path for 75 metres before broadening on a shelf of rock just before a junction, where we turn left, descending to the horseshoe lane linking **Targa** with the main road.

Fifty metres to the left, we leave the lane, turning right (Wp.3 20M) on a narrow concrete track that soon dwindles to a path. Bearing left at the corner of a solidly built wall, then right at the bottom of the wall, we cross a rocky slope to rejoin the horseshoe lane (Wp.4 25M). Turning left then right 50 metres later, we follow a tarmac lane (SE) past a dull orange house, 30 metres after which, immediately before a small quarry, we take a narrow path to the left marked with a cairn and, on the lamppost, the telephone number of the **Playa Santiago** taxi-station (Wp.5 30M), at which point you may wish to prepare yourself for the inevitable sharp intake of breath.

50 metres from the road, we go through a rock gateway and the view opens out (in every direction, most notably down) across the **Barranco de Guarimiar**, backed by **Teide** and (to our left) **Roque Agando**. Despite the dramatic drop, this is one of the more 'natural' cliff paths, unlike some where you get the impression some stubborn peasant just kept bludgeoning his way through till something akin to a path appeared in his wake. Heading north-east, we pass under impressive crags, where we come to the first slightly vertiginous stretch

before reaching a small cave (Wp.6 35M). The path winds down, passing a solitary palm (Wp.7 40M), the first on the descent, after which another very slightly vertiginous stretch leads north-east to the next series of zigzags. Following a very steep chicane, we pass a line of palms and cross a patch of gritty dirt, where we see **Roque Agando** again (Wp.8 50M). More zigzags pass a shallow sloping cave, after which we cross a canal (Wp.9 60M), visible for much of the descent. The zigzags now tend south-east, as we edge toward a watershed that has its source at the start of our descent, passing below another cave (Wp.10 70M). Brushing aside dense overhanging palms, we follow then cross the watershed before descending to a T-junction behind a cabin on its right bank (Wp.11 85M).

Turning left and re-crossing the watershed, we climb gently then steadily up the flank of the ravine on an intermittently cobbled path, negotiating more encroaching palm and a collapsed terrace wall. Passing below crags, we come onto a broad ledge-path leading to a natural rock gateway (Wp.12 100M) above an abandoned house. The path drops down and levels out briefly, before narrowing and winding between prickly pear, passing directly in front of a ruin (Wp.13 105M) with a superb bread oven built into the overhanging rock behind it. 25 metres after the ruin, we ignore a slightly clearer path climbing to the left and continue straight ahead, weaving between agave, prickly pear and house-leeks to scramble up a watercourse onto the porch of the next ruin.

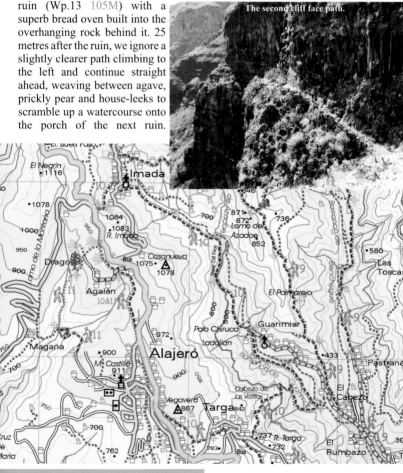

The second cliff face path.

Continuing in a northerly direction on a seriously embattled path, we descend to cross the **Guarimiar** watercourse, aiming for a grey metal pipe, where a faint way winds between the palms, crossing two terracing walls onto a dirt track (Wp.14 115M).

Turning left, we follow the dirt track till it ends below the highest **Guarimiar** houses and concrete steps lead onto another old path. The path runs into stained rocks at the bottom of a watershed, which we climb, taking the <u>second</u> turning on the right. Climbing steadily, we cross another watershed (Wp.15 130M) below cliffs patched with flat planes where fractured rock has yielded to gravity. Continuing our climb, we reach a canal, the same one crossed at Wp.9 (no, a shortcut would not be a clever idea!), below a water-chute so smoothly sculpted it looks like the mould for a concrete pipe. 50 metres later, we cross the canal (Wp.16 140M) and climb alongside a thin metal pipe before bearing right on steps in the rock, signalling the approach of another point where one wonders what on earth possessed anyone to think of making a path up here.

Climbing steadily on a broad ledge path, we traverse a <u>sheer</u> cliff face. Though this path, which is undeniably vertiginous, looks appalling in pictures and, from above, frankly terrifying (not recommended as a descent), it's never so narrow as to be seriously dangerous or downright foolhardy, and simply requires a little customary precaution. Picking our way carefully along it and resisting the temptation to peer over the edge, we spend about ten minutes traversing the actual cliff face, after which we wind up very steeply, coming into view of **Imada** (Wp.17 160M).

A clear path climbs to cross a sheet of rock, after which we come to a first Y-junction, the two branches rejoining 10 metres later. After crossing the second of two watersheds, the path is obscured by a long spill of rocks, at the top of which it becomes clearer again as it climbs to a very ruinous ruin (Wp.18 175M) immediately after which there's a second Y-junction. Once again, the two branches soon rejoin, but it's easier to take the left fork. At a third Y-junction a couple of minutes later, we branch left again, crossing rock onto a clear paved trail climbing steadily alongside a final watershed to the lower branch of the lane into **Imada** (Wp.19 190M).

Bearing right, we follow the lane to a transformer tower, where we turn left, winding between houses and ruins onto the upper lane. Bearing right again, we come to a discrete garage with dull red doors on our left and, on our right, a double garage with scarlet doors. Our path out of **Imada** starts on concrete steps (Wp.20 195M) climbing above the garage on the left to pass a ruin with a green door. 50 metres from the road, we bear right on reddish rock leading to an old paved path climbing between a small house and a hen coop to a 'Paisaje Protegido Orone' signpost. Climbing steeply, we pass a fine pine and the four-fingered salute of **Roque Imada**, before eventually crossing a canal and the ridge onto the main road (Wp.21 215M) 75 metres south of the **Almacigos** turn-off. We follow the road south for 400 metres to the second bend, where two paved trails branch right (Wp.22 220M). Taking the second trail, we descend to cross the **Agalán** lane (Wp.23 225M), where we join Walk 11 at Wp.7.

Dragon Trees (Dracaena draco, of the Yucca family) or *dragos*, which will probably be new to visitors unfamiliar with Hieronymous Bosch's 'Garden of Delights', are a distinctive part of Canarian flora, a survivor, like the *laurisilva* though considerably weirder, of the last ice-age. They've played an important part in traditional Canarian life, being attributed various medicinal properties that even extended to the political, the more venerable *dragos* functioning as symbolic parliaments in *guanche* times. Only having one wild example, Gomerans are tremendously proud of it, studiously marking it on even the sketchiest maps, carefully fencing it off, and laying a neat cobbled path so tourists can get to it. We, however, with the rambling perversity that inspired Chesterton's 'Rolling English Road', approach this distinguished tree from below, along an adventurous, pathless, riverbed route. This is the childish end of the walking spectrum, a chance to revisit cheerful times messing about in streams and precariously tottering between seaside rock pools.

**Access**: by car or bus ![bus] L2 or L6.
Motorists should park in front of the *Ayuntamiento*.

> **Stroll**
> **El Drago** from the parking area north of the **Imada** turn-off.

From the front of **Alajeró** church (Wp.1 0M), we cross the plaza toward a large Indian laurel where steps lead to a dirt track on the right, above the cemetery. Following the track west and bearing right at a Y-junction 100 metres later, we stroll into open countryside with fine views of the table-top **Fortaleza** (Walk 19) framed by the **Ermita de San Lorenzo** pass. The track then dips down, bringing us into view of the hamlet of **Magaña** before swinging right and ending on a grassy platform (Wp.2 10M).

Maintaining direction (ENE), we descend onto a donkey trail, leading down on a mixture of bare rock (mottled with an appealing camouflage of lichen), boulder paving, cobbles, and dirt (all of it slippery when wet) to the diminutive **Magaña** reservoir at the confluence of two wild ravines. Passing behind the reservoir into the second ravine, we ignore a broad donkey trail climbing to **Magaña** (from where we can stroll down to **Almacigos** – an attractive alternative excursion in spring when the wildflowers are out), and bear right on a faint goat trail (Wp.3 30M) leading toward a solitary palm. After climbing to the left of the palm, the goat trail drops down into the watercourse and, as goat trails tend to, promptly disappears, which is where the childish fun starts, hopping from boulder to boulder up the watercourse.

The *drago* in the rain.

There's no single way here, just a series of rocks interspersed with occasional patches of smooth gravel, but it's worth looking for cairns and the letter 'A'painted on the rocks. These are boundary markers rather than ramblers' waymarks, but presuming the landowner knew the easiest way along his property-line they're still helpful. Ignoring what appear to be old paths climbing to the right, we stick to the watercourse, soon coming to a first shallow channel of sandy coloured sedimentary rock where erosion has sculpted eye-catching whorls in the rock. After about 15M in the watercourse, we see the *drago* (up to our right and unmistakable) surrounded by green railings. Just as the *drago* disappears from sight, the watercourse deepens and narrows to a small gorge defined by sandy coloured bluffs and we bear right (Wp.4 50M), scrambling up a boulder-strewn gully onto a rough terrace path, 50 metres south of the *drago*. An easy climb across the terraces brings us to this hallowed tree (Wp.5 55M).

Skirting to the left of the railings, we climb onto a narrow well-paved path zigzagging steeply up toward the road. When the path crosses the end of a dirt track (Wp.6 70M), we turn right, following the dirt track to the northernmost house in the hamlet of **Agalán**, where we bear left on a narrow path running behind the house to the end of the tarmac access lane. Turning left, we follow the lane toward the main road, passing a fine old threshing circle and the easternmost house in the hamlet, 100 metres after which, at a line of palm trees, three tall, one short, we turn right on a broad cobbled trail running alongside a canal (Wp.7 80M). The trail narrows to an intermittently paved path that gradually bears away from the canal, eventually passing a new warehouse and emerging next to the bus-stop (Wp.8 90M) on the northernmost slip road into **Alajeró**. We follow this road back to our starting point.

(If you happen to be doing this route in reverse, the path from the bus-stop, which isn't obvious, runs to the left of the entrance to the warehouse).

An interesting and relatively easy alternative approach to **Garajonay** exploring the upper reaches of the **Barranco de Azadoe** and concluding with a spectacular descent. If you have an old map showing a route over the small wooded summit of **Eretos** (see Wp.9), ignore it! Cairns suggest this was once feasible, but it's now badly overgrown.

| 4 | 3 H | ➡ 12.5 km | 🏔 500m / 500m | ↻ | 🍴 1* |

* in **Imada**

**Short Version**
Linear descent from **Pajarito**, climbing to the **Imada** turn-off for the bus.

**Access**: by car & bus 🚌 L2 or L6. If arriving by bus L2, add 4 km return for the descent from the **Imada** turn-off. If arriving by bus L6, ask to be dropped off at the *carretera de* **Almacigos** and use the path described in Walk 10 Wps.21-20. Parking is limited, but there's usually room in front of the **Bar Arcilia** or at the end of the road.

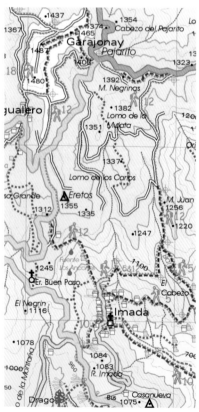

From the **Bar Arcilia** (Wp.1 0M), we climb very steeply to the end of the road (Wp.2 5M) where concrete and stone steps lead to a rough path crossing an affluent of the **Barranco de Azadoe**, after which superb views open out to the south. Climbing steadily, we cross a succession of minor spurs, each of which looks like it must be the last (but isn't!), until a series of partially paved zigzags brings us onto a ledge with stunning views into the **Barranco de Azadoe** (Wp.3 35M). From here, a gentle stroll along a level path, with one slightly vertiginous stretch, leads across the **Azadoe** watercourse to a junction (Wp.4 40M), where we turn left to climb alongside the watercourse.

Following a good, partially paved trail we climb steadily along the left bank of the ravine before bearing right and winding away from the watercourse. After a slightly steeper climb, the path levels off and, 50 metres later, passes a signpost for the 'Reserva

Natural de Benchijigua' (Wp.5 60M), from where we have excellent views of **Roque Agando**. We then enter the *Parque Nacional*, joining a dirt track, which we follow in a northerly direction, ignoring branches to left and right. After a gentle climb, we turn left on the *Carretera Dorsal* (Wp.6 85M) and follow the road for 50 metres to join a signposted path for 'Pajarito'. The path winds through bracken and *fayal-brezal*, climbing steadily to cross two small tops, after which a second stepped descent brings us onto a dirt track, where we bear right for the **Pajarito** parking area (Wp.7 105M), the starting point for the short version.

Crossing the **Igualero** road, we take the track circling the **Alto de Garajonay**.

**If you want to climb to the summit,**
- turn right immediately after the chain closing the track to cars (follow Walk 35, but turn left at Wp.2) and descend via the path used to reach the summit in Walk 18 (Wps. 15-13).

Otherwise, we stick to the dirt track circling the summit, eventually bearing left at a signposted branch for 'Igualero 1.8' (Wp.8 125M), just east of Walk 18 Wp.13. This track brings us down to the **Igualero-Chipude** road (Wp.9 135M) 100 metres west of the junction with the **Playa Santiago** road, which we follow (S) for 750 metres.

When the **Playa Santiago** road swings sharp right towards a dry dam seen on our way down, we turn left on a narrow dirt path (Wp.10 145M) defined by low gateway walls and flanked by dirt tracks. After crossing a track leading to a small house on our left, we bear left at an apparent Y-junction (the branch on the right is actually a watercourse), after which we see **Imada**.

Descending steeply between scorched cistus and broom, we reach a rocky spur crossed by a metal water pipe (Wp.11 155M), where we bear left (NE), winding down through increasingly invasive shrubs. The path gradually curves round to the south on a slightly gentler gradient to a canal beside a roofless cabin (Wp.12 165M), from where a straightforward descent on a long, shallow spur brings us into the village 50 metres above our starting point.

Superb views over Imada on route.

See the notes on GPS use and waypoints on page 18.

### 5. BARRANCO & LOMO DE AZADOE

| Wp | N | W |
|---|---|---|
| 1 | 28 05.1558 | 17 14.4948 |
| 2 | 28 05.0964 | 17 14.2470 |
| 3 | 28 05.0148 | 17 13.9230 |
| 4 | 28 05.0790 | 17 13.7742 |
| 5 | 28 04.9332 | 17 13.6458 |
| 6 | 28 05.2668 | 17 13.9908 |
| 7 | 28 05.3208 | 17 14.0358 |
| 8 | 28 05.4354 | 17 14.0994 |

### 6. JERDUNE - JARDIN TECINA

| Wp | N | W |
|---|---|---|
| 1 | 28 05.6748 | 17 11.3988 |
| 2 | 28 05.5314 | 17 11.1894 |
| 3 | 28 05.0478 | 17 10.9650 |
| 4 | 28 04.7886 | 17 10.7904 |
| 5 | 28 04.7808 | 17 10.5324 |
| 6 | 28 04.4760 | 17 10.5144 |
| 7 | 28 04.1682 | 17 10.5510 |
| 8 | 28 03.8718 | 17 10.4436 |
| 9 | 28 03.7644 | 17 10.4850 |
| 10 | 28 03.5148 | 17 10.4832 |
| 11 | 28 02.9406 | 17 10.7100 |
| 12 | 28 02.8542 | 17 10.7844 |
| 13 | 28 02.4942 | 17 11.0358 |
| 14 | 28 02.2896 | 17 10.8816 |
| 15 | 28 02.1588 | 17 11.1288 |
| 16 | 28 01.8738 | 17 11.4270 |

### 7. LAS TOSCAS - DEGOLLADA DE PERAZA

| Wp | N | W |
|---|---|---|
| 1 | 28 04.6428 | 17 12.5268 |
| 2 | 28 05.6034 | 17 12.9594 |
| 3 | 28 05.5416 | 17 13.1430 |
| 4 | 28 06.1050 | 17 12.9258 |
| 5 | 28 06.4110 | 17 12.8982 |
| 6 | 28 06.4542 | 17 12.8208 |

### 8. PLAYA SANTIAGO - TARGA

| Wp | N | W |
|---|---|---|
| 1 | 28 01.7292 | 17 11.8134 |
| 2 | 28 02.0508 | 17 12.1620 |
| 3 | 28 02.1138 | 17 12.0660 |
| 4 | 28 02.4516 | 17 12.5070 |
| 5 | 28 02.8272 | 17 12.7134 |
| 6 | 28 02.9958 | 17 13.1748 |
| 7 | 28 03.3822 | 17 13.2516 |
| 8 | 28 03.5460 | 17 13.6368 |
| 9 | 28 03.3204 | 17 13.5804 |
| 10 | 28 03.1098 | 17 13.6026 |
| 11 | 28 03.0318 | 17 13.6164 |
| 12 | 28 02.8218 | 17 13.6386 |
| 13 | 28 02.4456 | 17 13.2732 |
| 14 | 28 02.0586 | 17 12.7002 |
| 15 | 28 01.7958 | 17 12.1212 |

### 9. BARRANCO DE BENCHIJIGUA

| Wp | N | W |
|---|---|---|
| 1 | 28 03.3822 | 17 12.6336 |
| 2 | 28 03.7194 | 17 12.9834 |
| 3 | 28 04.0782 | 17 13.1370 |
| 4 | 28 04.1226 | 17 13.2150 |
| 5 | 28 04.1844 | 17 13.2096 |
| 6 | 28 04.3398 | 17 13.2846 |
| 7 | 28 04.5864 | 17 13.3824 |
| 8 | 28 04.8450 | 17 13.5606 |
| 9 | 28 05.1408 | 17 13.3470 |
| 10 | 28 05.3814 | 17 13.3098 |
| 11 | 28 05.5362 | 17 13.1430 |
| 12 | 28 05.4372 | 17 12.9150 |
| 13 | 28 05.1570 | 17 12.8562 |
| 14 | 28 04.8732 | 17 12.9318 |
| 15 | 28 04.6398 | 17 12.9258 |
| 16 | 28 04.3290 | 17 12.9678 |
| 17 | 28 04.0392 | 17 12.8820 |

### 10. BARRANCO DE GUARIMIAR

| Wp | N | W |
|---|---|---|
| 1 | 28 03.8346 | 17 14.3730 |
| 2 | 28 03.6030 | 17 14.1282 |
| 3 | 28 03.5616 | 17 13.8594 |
| 4 | 28 03.5814 | 17 13.7442 |
| 5 | 28 03.5508 | 17 13.6122 |
| 6 | 28 03.6606 | 17 13.5354 |
| 7 | 28 03.7074 | 17 13.5324 |
| 8 | 28 03.7806 | 17 13.4448 |
| 9 | 28 03.8256 | 17 13.3866 |
| 10 | 28 03.8250 | 17 13.3062 |
| 11 | 28 03.7344 | 17 13.1292 |
| 12 | 28 03.9702 | 17 13.3476 |
| 13 | 28 03.9996 | 17 13.4670 |
| 14 | 28 04.0716 | 17 13.5246 |
| 15 | 28 04.2870 | 17 13.6998 |
| 16 | 28 04.4526 | 17 13.8114 |
| 17 | 28 04.6878 | 17 13.8108 |
| 18 | 28 04.8444 | 17 14.2086 |
| 19 | 28 04.9560 | 17 14.4582 |
| 20 | 28 05.0412 | 17 14.4642 |
| 21 | 28 04.8564 | 17 14.6334 |
| 22 | 28 04.6524 | 17 14.5782 |
| 23 | 28 04.5060 | 17 14.4780 |

### 11. EL DRAGO

| Wp | N | W |
|---|---|---|
| 1 | 28 03.8076 | 17 14.4258 |
| 2 | 28 04.0434 | 17 14.7570 |
| 3 | 28 04.2012 | 17 14.8542 |
| 4 | 28 04.4202 | 17 14.8230 |
| 5 | 28 04.5006 | 17 14.8050 |
| 6 | 28 04.5300 | 17 14.6754 |
| 7 | 28 04.5036 | 17 14.4786 |
| 8 | 28 04.1766 | 17 14.3460 |

### 12. IMADA - GARAJONAY

| Wp | N | W |
|---|---|---|
| 1 | 28 05.1690 | 17 14.4936 |
| 2 | 28 05.2380 | 17 14.4450 |
| 3 | 28 05.2782 | 17 14.1012 |
| 4 | 28 05.4318 | 17 14.0868 |
| 5 | 28 05.7420 | 17 14.0886 |
| 6 | 28 06.4206 | 17 14.0004 |
| 7 | 28 06.4986 | 17 14.5038 |
| 8 | 28 06.2442 | 17 14.8536 |
| 9 | 28 05.8662 | 17 14.9460 |
| 10 | 28 05.5686 | 17 14.8602 |
| 11 | 28 05.4318 | 17 14.7018 |
| 12 | 28 05.3466 | 17 14.5914 |

From the *mirador* at **Igualero**'s *ermita*, you have a view of the grand landscapes ahead, but nothing will prepare you for your first drop into **Valle Gran Rey**. Winding along the country road past **Fortaleza** (Walk 19) and through the '1,000 metre' villages of **Chipude**, **Cercado** and **Las Hayas,** it is all rural bucolic charm, mixed with a degree of affluence evidenced by restored cottages, glitzy pick-ups and bar/restaurants. Dropping down to **Arure** take a short detour to the *ermita* for the stunning views down to **Taguluche**; Walk 25 explores this awesome landscape. Now for your first arrival in **Valle Gran Rey**.

From **Arure** the **Barranco de Arure** plunges down beside the road as we speed into the first tunnel. Down and down, to emerge on a broad carriageway curving steeply down past the César Manrique *mirador* to plunge through a hairpin bend (another *mirador*) into the second tunnel. Ahead is the sheer cliff wall as we emerge into the light to look down on the settlements high up the valley floor. Matchbox models resolve into full size houses as we drop steeply down through hairpin bends, rounding the church before reaching the first settlements. Even now it is still steeply down the valley between the towering cliff walls, sweeping through **Retamal**, **Los Granados**, **Casa La Seda** and **El Guro** before the slope runs out at **La Calera**. What a descent, and that is on the 'new' road. Stretches of the old road can be seen, and it is no surprise to find that it was nicknamed the 'screaming route' from the noise made by day trippers as their driver flung his coach into the tortuous descent.

By comparison **La Calera** and the sea front developments of **La Playa**, **La Puntilla** and **Vueltas** are peaceful tranquility. Once the preserve of hippies and adventurers, including Vietnam draft dodgers, La Gomera's main resort is becoming quite middle class, with new hotels and apartments attracting families where once camper vans ruled. Despite the modern developments, **Vueltas** and **La Calera** still retain a lot of character and even with the sea front tourism this is still a laid-back charming place to be based. Seekers after the au-naturel hippy lifestyle only have to hike north or south of the resort area to the cossie-optional beaches of **Playa del Ingles** and **Las Salinas** which are just as they always were.

Framed by the immense cliff walls, **Valle Gran Rey** presents some challenging walking routes, but you can opt for easier alternatives by bussing out of the valley and walking back; see Walk 16 from **Arure** and the second part of Walk 17. While the walking is challenging, you will be well rewarded in the *tipicos* that many of the walking routes call in at, and for days when you don't want to be challenged, the island's best beaches are just a stroll away.

A perfect introduction to everything good about La Gomera: friendly people, idyllic countryside, fairy tale forests, tiny hamlets and, at the end of it all, a good lunch!

**Stroll**
**Arure – Acardece**. Turn left on the track above the **Acardece** reservoir and follow the end of the walk from the 175M point.

**Short Version**
**Las Hayas – Las Creces**. Starting from the **Las Hayas** *ermita*, turn right at Wp.13 and follow the dirt track back to Wp.9

**Access**: by car and bus  L1 or L6

Our itinerary starts 20 metres south-west of the **Bar Conchita** bus-stop (Wp.1 0M) on a paved trail descending into the valley below **Arure**. After crossing a dry watercourse and a rock shelf flecked with carved steps, we bear left behind a white house on a path alongside a reservoir (Wp.2 10M). Bearing left again at the head of the reservoir, we cross bare rock (NE) to pick up another path along the southern flank of the **Arure** valley. The path joins a dirt track (Wp.3 15M), which we follow to the dam behind **Acardece**. Staying on the track as it passes the **Acardece** reservoir, a murky pond spotted with white ducks, we cross a small rise and turn right at a T-junction.

The track runs into concrete, immediately after which, we bear right at a Y-junction (Wp.4 30M). Ignoring three left-hand branches, the third of which is another Y-junction (Wp.5 35M), we cross a stream bed and join a donkey trail climbing the **Cabeza de la Vizcaina**. After a steady climb, we turn left on a dirt track (Wp.6 50M), passing a small yellow house and a branch to the left. Still climbing, we see the table-top summit of **Fortaleza** (Walk 19), then **Las Hayas**.

The track descends past a scruffy farmstead, then climbs toward the village, where it's roughly asphalted. 20 metres from the main road, we take the second of twin dirt tracks branching left (Wp.7 65M) to emerge higher up the road in front of the **Casa Efigenia** restaurant. Bearing left for 'Las Creces', we follow a tarmac driveway to a garage with green doors, where a path climbs between houses to a dirt track behind the **Ermita de Hayas**.

The track soon dwindles to a narrow path (Wp.8 75M) sandwiched between terraces and the edge of the *laurisilva*. Bearing right at a Y-junction a minute later, we enter classic Gomeran woodland, a carpet of sun-dappled leaf mould shrouded by a canopy of contorted lichen-bearded laurel and heath trees. The path descends gently to cross a dirt track (Wp.9 85M), where we see the first of the numbered posts for the park's 'self-guider' walk (see Introduction).

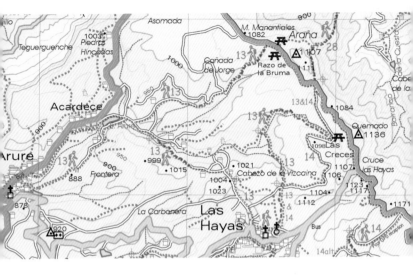

After a steadier, partially stepped descent into a densely wooded gully, we cross an affluent (Wp.10 90M) and stroll through increasingly lush forest. Ignoring a branch to the left for **Arure** (Wp.11 95M), we continue on the main path (N), climbing gently to cross another gully (Wp.12 100M). Following the right bank of the gully, we criss-cross an ancient canalisation channel, climbing gently to the *área recreativa* at **Las Creces** (Wp.13 110M). *Creces* are the berries of *haya*, which means beech on the mainland, but is used here for the Canary wax-myrtle. In the past, the people of **Las Hayas** came here to collect the *creces*, once an important part of the local diet.

Bearing left, we take the *área recreativa* access track up to the main road (Wp.14 115M), which we follow (NW) for 800 metres to the small picnic area behind **Araña**, where we turn left on a trail signposted 'Cañada de Jorge' (Wp.15 125M).

*Laurisilva* forest at Las Creces.

### Alternatively

- to avoid most of the road, there's a roundabout but more picturesque route. Turning right 50 metres north-west of Wp.14, we follow the 'Vallehermoso 5.8' path down to the 'Raso de la Bruma 0.7' junction. Turning left, we climb through enchanting woodland and rejoin the road in front of Wp.15 (135M, add 10M to all subsequent times).

The **Cañada de Jorge** trail descends through dense woodland to join the end of a track leading to the main *pista forestal* (Wp.16 140M) from the road. Bearing left, we follow the *pista* out of the park into scrubby *fayal-brezal*. After briefly dwindling to a walking trail, the *pista* broadens again to a hard-baked dirt track, which we follow (W) towards a large white house, where we join a tarmac lane (Wp.17 150M). Maintaining direction (W), we follow the lane back to Wp.4 (175M).

Staying on the main track as it circles the **Acardece** reservoir, we turn left 50 metres after the dam wall and descend a metalled track (Wp.18 180M), at the end of which a newly paved path winds through the hamlet before joining the road (Wp.19 185M). 30 metres along the road, another paved trail branches left back into the valley and open countryside. When this trail switches back sharp left, we continue in a south-westerly direction on a narrow path. Sticking to the main path and ignoring all branches, we come to another newly paved stretch, which rejoins the road 50 metres from our starting point (195M). Conchita's *carne fiesta* (chunks of fried pork marinated in vinegar, lemon juice, cumin and bay leaves) is particularly recommended.

# 14. LAS CRECES – ROUNDABOUT ROUTE

A walk that can be neatly divided into five distinct phases: first, the popular and dramatic trail crossing the **Barrancos del Agua** and **de las Lagunetas** between **Las Hayas** and **El Cercado**; second, a virtually unknown and consequently overgrown trail recrossing the same ravines higher up; third, the lovely mixed woodland climbing from the **Barranco de las Lagunetas**; fourth, the unlovely but tolerable *Carretera Dorsal*; and fifth, the classic *laurisilva/fayal-brezal* forest between **Las Creces** and **Las Hayas**.

| Stroll **Las Hayas** to **Cercado** (see text) | 🍽️ **Casa Efigenia** aka **La Montañeta**, isn't exactly *tipico* since it's become so famous only tourists use it nowadays, but it's still worth a visit, especially for despairing vegetarians. Be prepared to wait, though. Fast Food is the only thing not *de la casa*. If you don't want to linger, **Bar Amparo** is where the locals go for a fine *carne de cabra*. |
|---|---|
| **Short Version** see Wp.8 | |

**Access**: by car and bus 🚌 L1, L6 or L7. Motorists should park on the **Ermita de las Hayas** access lane and descend through the village to **Bar Amparo**. The **Las Hayas** bus-stop is at the junction with the **Cercado** road: add 800 metres return to **Bar Amparo**.

Taking the stepped path to the right of **Bar Amparo** (Wp.1 5M), we descend to a Y-junction of dirt tracks and bear left on the lower track, which is in the process of being asphalted. Curving round the **Revolcadero** valley, we climb onto a small ridge, where we cross a tarmac lane (Wp.2 10M) and take a well-trodden path to the left of a long, low building with a red roof. Bearing left at a Y-junction 50 metres later, we traverse largely abandoned terraces before climbing to join another path (Wp.3 20M) within sight of **El Cercado** and the table-top **Fortaleza**. Maintaining our south-easterly direction for 50 metres, we reach the lip of the **Lagunetas** and **Agua** ravines. Bearing left on a broad ledge, we wind down to cross the **Lagunetas** watercourse (Wp.4 30M) then traverse a terraced slope to the **Agua** watercourse (Wp.5 35M).

**For the stroll to El Cercado**
We continue on the donkey trail climbing the southern flank of the ravine, bearing left after a couple of minutes to stay on the cobbled trail. We emerge on the main road in front of **Bar/Restaurante Maria** (Wp.6 45M), from where we can either return via the same route or use Maria's taxi driving brother (tel. for both restaurant and taxi: 922-804-034 or 922-804-167).

**For the main walk**
We bear left at Wp.5, crossing an outcrop of rock onto a dirt track, which we follow up the valley to the road (Wp.7 45M). Turning left, we follow the road for 30 metres then cross onto a dirt track climbing toward a stone cabin. 15

metres from the road, we branch left toward a palm grove some 50 metres to the north. At first it seems we are walking into pathless scrub, but a few metres from the track, we bear right in front of a stunted fig tree and find ourselves on the remains of a cobbled trail overgrown with cistus and broom. Once on the trail, it's easy to follow as it crosses two subsidiary ridges of the **Lomo de la Pecena**, bringing us into view of **Valle Gran Rey**. The trail clears as we descend under a shady canopy of heath trees to a Y-junction (Wp.8 65M) where we bear left, re-crossing the **Lagunetas** watercourse to join a dirt track.

## For the short version
Bear left and follow the dirt track down to the **Cercado-Hayas** road, 1.3 km from the **Las Hayas** bus stop

## For the full walk
We cross the dirt track and continue on the donkey trail, climbing briefly before the trail levels out in deeper, denser, darker woodland. Joining a dirt track (Wp.9 75M), we swing right, initially SSE, but gradually bearing ENE, climbing steadily then gently through the woods to the *Carretera Dorsal* (Wp.10 85M).

Bearing left, we follow the road for a little under two kilometres. Cars are few but fast, so stay on the left and take care at sharp bends. I hesitate to mention this, but there's a lovely forestry path climbing from **Las Creces** and petering out a mere 50 metres from **Cruce Las Hayas**. Unfortunately, those 50 metres are such a maze of interlacing gullies and tangled woodland it's best to stick to the road for another ten minutes to the signposted dirt track (Wp.11 105M) down to the *área recreativa* at **Las Creces** (Wp.12 115M). Continuing on the dirt track for 'Las Hayas 2.6', we stroll through lovely woodland, eventually turning left on a path signposted 'Las Hayas 0.7' (Wp.13 130M). A gentle climb through the woods brings us to the **Ermita de las Hayas** (Wp.14 135M), where we bear left to return to the starting point.

Most people arrive in **Valle Gran Rey** by road, which is dramatic but bruising, abruptly dropping down 1000 metres to a resort that is being redeveloped so rapidly it looks like they're dismantling it. Arriving on foot by the old donkey trail from **Cercado** is an infinitely more spacious, gracious and comfortable approach, letting us appreciate just why this was such a haven for hippies in the sixties. Even the 'dismantled' bits at the bottom reveal themselves in a kindlier light, not as the nearest thing (not very near in all honesty) La Gomera has to Tenerife-style tourism, but as a nucleus of quality services with a couple of good bathing beaches. In short, an ideal introduction to one of the classic walking areas of La Gomera. The high exertion rating is all in the knees. There's a slight risk of vertigo between **Cercado** and **Vizcaina**.

Access: by bus 🚌 L1, L6, L7

**Stroll**
Bus to the **Vizcaina** turn-off and follow the road round to join the walk at Wp.6

**Short Version**
Turn right at Wp.6 to the bus-stop at the **Vizcaina** turn-off

Directly in front of the **Bar/Restaurante Maria** (Wp.1 0M), we take the lane (W) along the ridge between the **Barrancos del Agua** and **Matanza**, soon coming into sight of **Vizcaina**. After the last house in **Cercado**, the lane becomes a dirt track, 100 metres along which, just before a small farm, we bear right on a broad donkey trail marked with cairns and a '*Parque Rural*' signpost (Wp.2 5M).

From here to **Vizcaina** we simply follow the donkey trail through successive stretches of zigzagging descent and level 'balcony' paths. There are no major turn-offs, so if you're not interested in pacing progress, close the book for the next hour. After following the rim of the ravine with spectacular views back towards the dry falls at the confluence of the **Barrancos de las Lagunetas** and **del Agua**, we start our descent, ignoring a minor dirt path branching to the left and staying on the main trail, which is roughly paved and stepped with boulders. Zigzagging down, we pass a painted rock (Wp.3 20M) and traverse the first 'balcony'.

After a second series of zigzags, we pass a plump, solitary palm and come to the second balcony, at the end of which views open out along **Valle Gran Rey**. We then descend past a small stagnating spring (Wp.4 40M) onto the third balcony, after which we cross a rockspill and resume our steady descent onto a fourth balcony. An eroded stretch descends past a small, abandoned reservoir, backed by a single tall palm and fronted by terraces densely packed with shorter palms (Wp.5 60M), after which we cross a canal onto a newly resurfaced path. Descending past houses on the periphery of **Vizcaina**, we emerge next to a phone booth on the lane linking the villages of **Valle Gran**

**Rey** (Wp.6 70M).

We follow the lane down the valley, branching left when the main lane swings right towards 'Los Granados' (Wp.7 85M). At the end of the branch lane (Wp.8 90M), we take a surfaced path to the right, passing the **Casa de Chele**. The path descends past a semi-troglodytic cabin before passing in front of a larger house, where the modern paving ends, giving way to successive stretches of cobbles and dirt. After **Casa los Reyes** (Wp.9 100M), we ignore branch paths to the **Casa Luna** and donkey sanctuary, and cross the plaza in front of the **Ermita los Reyes**, at the far end of which a newly surfaced trail descends onto the dirt track in the bed of the valley (Wp.10 105M).

"... views open out along Valle Gran Rey ..."

The trail continues up to **El Guro**, but we turn left and follow the rather scruffy dirt track down the riverbed, bearing left twice when the main traces curve up to the road, eventually emerging in the new bus station (Wp.11 130M). Services and taxis can be found to the right in **La Calera**, services and bathing to the left in **Vueltas**.

# 16. LA MÉRICA

There are many valid reasons for rambling. Some walk to exercise, some to escape, some to explore, some to see. This long descent is for the last category, taking in some of the most spectacular views on the island. It's a popular walk, often treated as an ascent, apparently premised on the assumption that sweat equals merit. At Discovery Walking Guides we take a more leisurely, less moralising attitude! Though abrupt, the descent is well-graded, hence the low exertion rating.

Access: by bus 🚌 L1 or L6

**Stroll**
To the *mirador*, 100 metres after the turn-off

**Short Version**
To the first ruin after Wp.4

Starting in **Arure** from the **Bar Conchita** bus-stop (Wp.1 0M), we follow the road down towards **Valle Gran Rey** for 500 metres then turn right for the **Mirador Ermita del Santo**, which is currently (eternally, it would seem, given the financial problems the project has endured) being revamped. Following the road and then the dirt track past the *mirador*, we soon reach toe-curling views, first from the end of the tarmac into the **Barranco de Arure** then, 100 metres along the track, down to **Taguluche**. Climbing past the path (Wp.2 20M) from **Taguluche** (see Walk 25), we see the **Mérica** ridge and, doubtless, a few diabolic whiffs of smoke from the town rubbish tip. After passing a neat goat pen, the track curves round to the dump and we maintain our south-westerly direction on a narrower track (Wp.3 30M) signposted, without apparent irony, a 'protected natural area'. A little over 100 metres later, we leave the track, branching right on a paved trail waymarked 'VGR'.

And that, if you don't like consulting a guidebook when you're walking, is all you need to know. The rest of the trail is broad, easy and obvious, with fabulous views across the *barrancos* and out to sea, and no major turn-offs. The paving soon gives way to a dirt trail, climbing steadily, to pass above a second, scruffier goat pen, after which it levels out as a ridge path, with superb views only marred by the mound of rubbish spilling down the hillside to our right.

Dropping down below a third goat pen, we run into a broad, very slightly vertiginous ledge path, lined with partially walled caves redolent of goats. Ignoring a minor branch (Wp.4 50M) climbing right to the **Mérica** trig point, we begin our first, gentle descent across a plateau that must once have been the bread basket of western La Gomera. We then pass a block of rock, capped with tiny stone totems left by the pioneering hippies that popularised La Gomera, tucked behind which are the ruins of a substantial stone house. After passing between a second ruin and an immense, starred threshing circle (Wp.5 65M), we come to a Y-junction (Wp.6 75M) marked by four tattered sacking flags. The path to the right is a short excursion to the **Riscos de la**

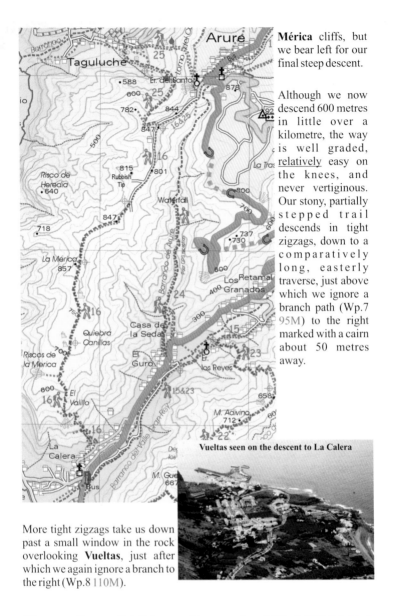

**Mérica** cliffs, but we bear left for our final steep descent.

Although we now descend 600 metres in little over a kilometre, the way is well graded, relatively easy on the knees, and never vertiginous. Our stony, partially stepped trail descends in tight zigzags, down to a comparatively long, easterly traverse, just above which we ignore a branch path (Wp.7 95M) to the right marked with a cairn about 50 metres away.

**Vueltas seen on the descent to La Calera**

More tight zigzags take us down past a small window in the rock overlooking **Vueltas**, just after which we again ignore a branch to the right (Wp.8 110M).

We eventually enter **La Calera** next to a map board (Wp.9 125M) behind apartments topped with gaily painted water tanks and fronted by a reservoir so weedy it resembles a lawn. Bearing right and right again at the next junction, we pass the **Bar/Restaurante/Zumeria El Mirador**, after which the road is pedestrianised. Branching left past the **Restaurante El Descansillo**, we descend to the taxi-rank and old bus-stop in front of the *Ayuntamiento* (Wp.10 135M).

Looking at this one from below, it's hard to believe there's a way up the **Barranco de Hayas**. Considerable suspension of disbelief is required en route, too, as we climb incredibly steeply, traversing several vertiginous ledge paths. But there is a way, one strenuous enough to make getting to the top even more of a feel-good moment than usual. You need to be fit, though, and have a good head for heights, not to mention a faintly masochistic taste for the more gruelling side of walking. By contrast, the descent is pure pleasure and within the capacity of any walker with reasonably robust knees.

Access: by car and bus L1 or L6.

The walk starts from the bus-stop at the **Lomo del Balo/Vizcaina** turn-off, where there's also a small parking area.

**Strolls**
**Hayas** to the *mirador* just before Wp.12

**Short Versions**
Bus to **Hayas** and do the descent

**Extension**
Turn left on the **Vizcaina** road and descend to **La Calera** (see Walk 15)

Following the **Vizcaina** road for 100 metres, we cross two watercourses and turn left into the second, the **Barranco de Hayas** (Wp.1 2M), on a faint, grassy path (NOT on the main paved path 5 metres beyond the watercourse). Ignoring a path onto terraces to the left, we climb directly up the watercourse for 50 metres before a dirt path bears left, bringing us onto a <u>very</u> steep cobbled path. Once you've found the path, it's simply a question of keeping on keeping on, climbing and climbing and climbing, and ignoring all apparent branches. If in doubt look for lines of stones blocking branch 'paths' and cairns indicating the correct way on the mainly stone-laid trail.

After climbing between terraces, we cross a canal, where we ignore an apparent branch to the left up a rockspill, and continue up a steep spur. Toward the top of the spur (Wp.2 20M), the gradient eases briefly and we ignore another apparent branch to the right. Climbing steeply again, we cross the head of the spur, bearing away from the **Barranco de Hayas** watercourse, before climbing across bare, reddish-brown rock to a T-junction below low crags (Wp.3 30M). Turning left (W) on the main stepped path, we come to our first slightly vertiginous section followed by another steep, winding climb to the top of a watershed, where we cross five steps carved in the rock (Wp.4 35M).

Bearing right (E), again on a gentler gradient, we climb past a tiny cave, after which the path levels out for 75 metres, in so far as the rough terrain allows, and heads back towards the *barranco* on an occasionally vertiginous ledge. After climbing to cross the head of a second, more precipitous watershed, our path briefly levels off before resuming its remorseless ascent. Rounding a bend (Wp.5 50M), we see the falls at the head of the *barranco*, at which point we ignore traces carrying straight on and bear sharp left. Zigzagging up with dizzying rapidity, we cross a stone wall blocking the path (Wp.6 55M), after which we traverse two vertiginous ledges, and come to two more winding ascents interrupted by a long more or less level shelf. After one last vertiginous stretch, the way broadens, passing shallow caves as it approaches the head of the *barranco*, before finally bearing left (N) on a mixture of bare rock and overgrown path (pathfinding's slightly tricky here – look for the cairns) to join a rough rocky trail (Wp.7 70M) within sight of the **Hayas-Arure** road.

Bearing right, we follow the trail east, crossing the end of a dirt track leading to a small house above the falls. Our trail widens to a stony track (later asphalted), which we follow all the way to the road (Wp.8 85M). Turning right, we follow the road round a long bend, after which we branch right on a dirt track. When the track forks, we continue on the right hand branch, which bears right after 10 metres toward two new houses, at which point we carry straight on, following a narrow path behind the houses. The land between the new houses and the road is subject to redevelopment, so the surface though not the general direction of the next 200 metres may change. At present the narrow path leads to a broad trail which in turn joins a dirt track that runs into tarmac shortly before joining the main road.

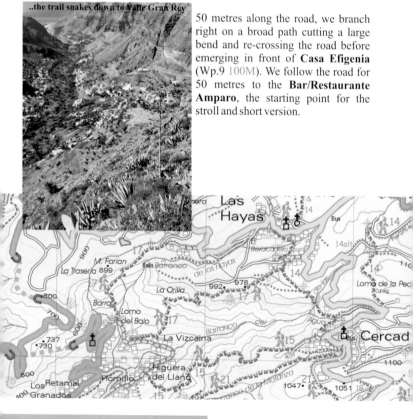

..the trail snakes down to Valle Gran Rey

50 metres along the road, we branch right on a broad path cutting a large bend and re-crossing the road before emerging in front of **Casa Efigenia** (Wp.9 100M). We follow the road for 50 metres to the **Bar/Restaurante Amparo**, the starting point for the stroll and short version.

Taking the stepped descent beside **Bar Amparo**, we cross the **Revolcadero** ridge (see Walk 14 Wps.1-2 for details), 50 metres beyond which, we take the right hand fork at a Y-junction of walking trails (Wp.10 110M), marked with blue and red dots. Ignoring all branches, we follow the main trail across a small rise, where we pass a signpost for the 'Parque Rural Valle Gran Rey' (Wp.11 115M). Continuing west, we come to one of the finest natural *miradors* overlooking **Valle Gran Rey**, soon after which we begin our descent (Wp.12 120M).

There are several great descents into the 'Valley of the Great King', but for head on impact (I'm speaking metaphorically here!), this is probably the greatest. The trail is very steep, but very well made and never vertiginous. You don't want to be reading a book here. Just walk and enjoy. There's nowhere you can really go wrong unless you actively choose to do so! The only point at which you might be momentarily confused comes at a rockspill after 15M descending, where the path appears to divide. We bear left, the branch to the right ending after a few metres.

The trail eventually passes under power cables and drops down amid a dense grove of palm onto the head of a long spur (Wp.13 150M), itself considerably steeper than it looks from above. Descending directly along the back of the spur, we pass a small house and cross a canal, after which we come to a Y-junction (Wp.14 165M).

Terraces in Valle Gran Rey

Both ways descend to the road, but since your knees have probably had enough sheer descent for one day, I suggest bearing right to a broad terrace path (clearly visible from above), joining the road 75 metres from the **Bar Lomo del Balo**, five minutes from the start of the walk. If the **Bar Lomo del Balo** is shut or you want to eat, turn left on the road and descend to the **Bar-Bodegon Vizcaina**, a little over ten minutes away.

# 18. CHIPUDE - GARAJONAY

An off-beat approach to the summit of **Garajonay**, using the network of dirt tracks and donkey trails behind **Chipude** and **Cercado**. The route is exposed, so can be a bit hot and dusty, but by the same token the views are consistently good.

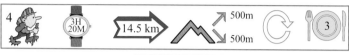

**Access**: by bus 🚌 L1, L6 or L7, or car.

> **Short Versions**
> **(a) Chipude – Cruce de Maria** loop
> **(b)** from the **Las Tajoras Casa Forestal** drive to **Cruce de Maria** and climb from Wp.10

Starting on the slip lane behind the phone booth opposite **Bar Navarro** in **Chipude**'s main square (Wp.1 0M), we cross a cobbled lane and take a broad concrete path (N) next to a pale pink house. At the end of the path, steps descend to a rough track leading to a green building. Crossing the track, we swing left on a dirt path, descending briefly along the left bank of a dry watercourse before turning right at a breeze-block byre. Crossing onto the right bank, we traverse a rock shelf lined with prickly pear and descend to the main road (Wp.2 7M), where we turn right. 50 metres after a breeze-block garage with blue doors, we turn left on a broad trail signposted 'Cercado' (Wp.3 10M) and cross the valley.

Crossing the road on the far side of the valley (Wp.4 15M), we continue climbing on the donkey trail till we see **Cercado**. Leaving the trail, we turn right on a dirt track (Wp.5 20M) passing the end of an asphalted branch from **Cercado**. Climbing east, we come into view of the antennae at the southern tip of **Garajonay** and, off to our right, the tiny hamlet of **Los Manantiales**. After a steady climb, the track passes under a water pipe at a staggered cross-roads (Wp.6 35M) and we turn sharp right to continue climbing along the ridge dividing the **Manantiales** and **Matanza** ravines.

Approaching a grove of rather beleaguered palm trees, the track levels off and we turn left on a narrow path marked by cairns (Wp.7 50M). Climbing between the palms and increasingly robust *fayal-brezal*, we emerge at the end of a minor dirt track (Wp.8 60M). When this track joins the **Tajoras** *pista forestal* (Wp.9 65M), we bear right and descend to the signposted junction at **Cruce de Maria** (Wp.10 70M)

**For short walk (a)**
Turn right here.

**For the full walk** and **short walk (b)**
Take the chained track east, signposted 'Alto de Garajonay'.

The **Garajonay** track curves away from a minor branch on our left and a stand of tall pine, **El Pinar de Argumame**, climbing steadily then steeply. Joining

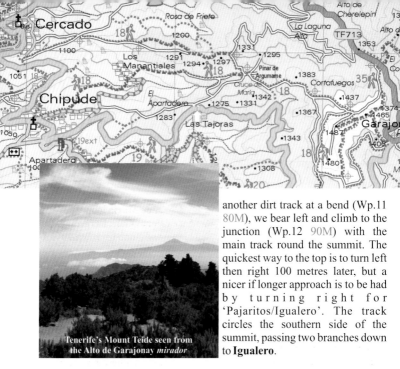

another dirt track at a bend (Wp.11 80M), we bear left and climb to the junction (Wp.12 90M) with the main track round the summit. The quickest way to the top is to turn left then right 100 metres later, but a nicer if longer approach is to be had by turning right for 'Pajaritos/Igualero'. The track circles the southern side of the summit, passing two branches down to **Igualero**.

*Tenerife's Mount Teide seen from the Alto de Garajonay mirador*

We take the first branch on the left (Wp.13 105M), a broad trail climbing through mixed woodland to a cross-roads of paths (Wp.14 115M). Turning left, we climb to the **Alto de Garajonay** *mirador* (Wp.15 120M), from where we have superb views of the neighbouring islands, notably Tenerife but also Gran Canaria on a clear day.

To return, we descend (S) past the firewatch cabin and take the **Contadero** dirt track - not the branch to the antennae. After turning left at the 'Chipude/Pajaritos' junction (Wp.16 125M), we rejoin our outward route, which we follow back to the **Cruce de Maria** turn-off (Wp.10 145M). Crossing the **Tajoras** *pista forestal* (also signposted 'Chipude'), we take the <u>path</u> for 'Chipude 1.8'. The path soon becomes a dirt track which in turn joins another dirt track, where we bear right. Carrying straight on (right) at a Y-junction (Wp.17 150M), we maintain a westerly direction as the increasingly rough track dwindles to a trail. The trail, littered with the rubble of collapsed retaining walls, gradually settles into a smooth dirt path descending to the end of the **Manantiales** access lane (Wp.18 175M).

The donkey trail to **Chipude** is clearly visible on the left flank of the valley, but first we bear right on a recently paved path to the older houses of the hamlet. At the first house, we turn left, as indicated by a red arrow on the wall, and descend between the house and animal pens to join a dirt path, where we bear left again. Ignoring a narrow branch to the right, we continue to the next house, where a steep cobbled path descends to cross the watercourse and join the clear trail (Wp.19 180M). A gentle to steady climb brings us onto a ridge (Wp.20 190M) just NE of **Chipude**, after which we cross a shallow swale and join the cobbled lane (Wp.21 195M) crossed at the beginning of the walk. Turning right, we follow this lane back to the main square.

# 19. FORTALEZA

The **Fortaleza** or 'fortress' is the distinctive table-top mountain seen from just about every key vantage point in the south-west. It's usually approached from **Chipude**, but we favour this circuit from the **Erque** turn-off. Though short, the walk involves some strenuous scrambling and a short chimney climb. There's a slight risk of vertigo, but the difficulty should not be exaggerated. We did it with a forty-kilo Old English Sheepdog in tow and were followed by a man with a baby on his back!

**Access**: by car and bus 🚌 L1 or L6 – ask for *carretera de* **Erque**, not an official stop, but there's room for the bus to pull over. Motorists can park above the reservoirs, 100 metres down the **Erque** road.

**Short Version**
Bear left at Wp.7, excluding the final climb

**Extension**: **Chipude** (see text)

Starting from the **Erque** turn-off (Wp.1 0M), we descend along the **Erque** road, passing two large reservoirs, 50 metres after which, we turn right onto an eroded donkey trail (Wp.2 5M). The trail drops down to cross a watercourse (Wp.3 10M) after which it continues as a dirt path skirting the northern flank of the valley behind the hamlet of **Apartadero**. It's worth pausing here to look at the **Fortaleza** and orient yourself: the white path through the green tonsure below the summit is our way into the rocks. Ignoring all branches, we stick to the main path as it descends into **Apartadero**, joining first another donkey trail then a tarmac slip road (Wp.4 20M) 100 metres east of the CEPSA petrol station. Turning left, we descend onto the **La Dama** road.

Following the road toward the head of the **Barranco de Iguala**, we bear right at the **Bar Los Camioneros** (Wp.5 25M) on a donkey trail cutting across the ravine. We rejoin the road in front of a bright yellow house (Wp.6 30M), 50 metres west of the cobbled lane to the shabbily picturesque hamlet of **Pavon**. After a steady climb, the lane runs into tarmac then dirt before dwindling to a donkey trail. Climbing past a neat but weather-beaten farmhouse (look at the stones pinning the tiles to the roof), we bear right at a Y-junction (Wp.7 35M) onto the saddle behind **Fortaleza**, where there's a '*Monumento Natural*' signpost.

Fortaleza

After a steady climb on a clear path, we come to the base of the white path (Wp.8 40M) and the climb steepens. 30 metres from two eucalyptus trees, 10 metres from a large red '2'on the rock, the white path swings left, climbing into the rocks defining the summit. Using partially tailored 'natural' steps, we reach a rough, sloping ledge and bear slightly right to a rock chimney (Wp.9 50M) identifiable by a faint green waymark and two small shelves of rubble, one halfway up, the other at the top.

After a very slightly vertiginous five-metre climb during which we have to steady ourselves with our hands, we emerge on a craggy ridge between the chimney and the summit. Taking care to memorise our route, which is less obvious on the way back, we wind through the rocks onto the sloping rim of the plateau, 50 metres east of a large white metal cross (Wp.10 60M). We now simply follow the cairns (SW) across the plateau to the trig-point (Wp.11 65M). The summit is a bit of an anticlimax after the chimney ascent, but the views are good, notably of the ravines around **La Dama**.

Retracing our steps to Wp.7 (85M), we have a choice of routes.

**If you arrived by car**
Bear right, maintaining direction (ENE) on a broad partially cobbled donkey trail that climbs steadily to join the **Erque** road 75 metres below the reservoirs (100M).

**If you're relying on the bus**
- and either have time to kill or don't trust the driver to acknowledge a sweaty rambler at an unscheduled stop, turn left and return to Wp.4 for the extension.

**Extension**
From Wp.4 (0M) follow the tarmac slip road down toward the petrol station and bear right 10 metres before the road on a concrete then cobbled trail climbing to a white house spotted with black stones. After passing in front of the house, we rejoin the road for 30 metres before branching right on a concrete track climbing to a bus stop (an alternative start, ask the driver for **Apartadero**) (Wp.12 5M), where we can either wait in the shade for the bus, or cross onto a signposted trail that rejoins the road 75 metres from **Chipude**'s (bar-lined!) square.

# 20. BARRANCO DE ERQUE

This long tour round one of the island's most spectacular and isolated ravines is by far the toughest walk in the book and only recommended in its entirety for experienced walkers with excellent pathfinding skills. For three quarters of the itinerary, there's not a smooth, straightforward step to be had. We descend on the sort of 'way' that makes you marvel at the intensity of old time neighbourly feeling - you really had to want to get at someone to beat a path down here. And the ascent follows the remains of a donkey trail that's a bit like Dr. Who's Tardis, in that it keeps disappearing at critical junctures of the narrative. In sum, the sort of walk which you end with a faint sense of incredulity, as it doesn't seem wholly feasible to have done all that in a single day. The final balcony path, Short Version (a), is recommended to everyone. Short Version (b) is recommended for adventurous, energetic walkers. The Full Version…read the text, you'll know who you are! There's a slight risk of vertigo and a strong risk of dehydration. Take at least 3 litres water per person, plus soft drinks and food. It's worth repeating, given the difficulty of this walk, that timings are 'pure', excluding all breaks and pathfinding pauses. Allow at least eight hours for the full walk.

**Short Versions**
**(a) Igualero** to **Chipude**. From the Igualero bus-stop, descend along the paved lane through the village for 500 metres then branch left on a blue waymarked path. Turn right at the T-junction to join the described itinerary at Wp.26. Descend from Wp.2 to Wp.3 then bear right to pick up the extension of Walk 19 to **Chipude**.
**(b)** take the dirt track/lane back from **Erquito** (see text)
**(c)** turn left at the junction after Wp.8 to join the path (see map) up from **Erque**.

**Extension**
See Walk 19 for access from the **Apartadero** bus-stop and **Chipude**

**Access**: see Walk 19. Motorists park at Wp.2, 300 metres down the **Erque** road or, to avoid a heartbreaking little climb at the end, Wp.27, 1 km down the **Erque** road.

From the **Erque** turn-off (Wp.1 0M), we follow the road for 300 metres till it swings sharp left (Wp.2 5M) and we continue straight ahead (SW) on a broad trail curving round a bend, from where we can see **Erquito**, the pine forested slopes below **Igualero**, and part of our final, balcony path. Our trail descends past a ruin, after which we branch left (Wp.3 15M) just before an inhabited farm. We pass above a second ruin (tiled roof) to a third ruin (corrugated iron roof and green door), where a large cairn indicates the start of a hugely improbable descent (Wp.4 16M). Whether this should be called a path or a 'way' is a moot point, but for the sake of convenience, I call it a path.

At first, the path is clear, crossing occasional steep rock steps and descending

Jeanette tackles the shelf descent.

(E) through a great sweep of agave and prickly pear, but after ten minutes, a slightly vertiginous stretch zigzags down a very steep slope onto a ledge where the way becomes unclear (Wp.5 35M). Bearing right for 20 metres, we pass above a small slightly unnerving drop until we see a curious wall built into the overhang beyond the watershed ahead of us.

On our left, a nub of rock, hopefully marked by a cairn, protrudes from the drop to form a small cleft wedged full of boulders. Edging onto the blocked cleft, we cross the face of the small drop on a naturally stepped shelf, at the bottom of which we recover the path. The rest of the descent is well-marked with cairns.

Bearing left, we follow a natural rock 'terrace' for 150 metres until a cairn indicates the way down onto the next 'terrace', after which the path becomes clearer as it winds down a steep rocky spur toward the great rhino-head ridge extending from the **Orilla de Amagra** - the tallest of the 'horns'. After traversing a long slab of rock between two dumpy palms (Wp.6 65M), we come to a slightly obscure stretch where sheep have trailblazed dozens of splinter 'paths' through the prickly pear. Bearing right (S), we stick to the cairn-marked way for a very steep descent off the nose of the rocky spur, after which a straightforward but still steep descent brings us to a watercourse feeding the ravine (Wp.7 90M). After crossing the watercourse, it's worth looking back at the descent: from here what seemed improbable from above is plainly impossible!

Branching right at a Y-junction 50 metres later, we follow a dirt path segmented by outcrops of rock, skirting the southern tip of the rhino-ridge

The 'duck and chick' rock pillars

before passing behind a grey bungalow, the 'Villagarcia' (Wp.8 100M). Passing below two small houses directly behind **Villagarcia**, we bear right at a junction, ignoring concrete steps up to the **Erque** dirt track. Descending towards the bed of the main *barranco* on a partially cobbled way, we reach a small spur tipped with a wooden electricity post and 'duck-and-chick' pillars of rock.

Leaving the main path, which descends to the right of the pillars, we cross the neck of rock <u>behind</u> them and drop <u>down</u> onto a narrow path descending (E) to pass between small terraces and tall, scorched palms. At the end of the lowest terrace, we bear right on an overgrown path descending to cross the stream (Wp.9 110M), beyond which we climb over a terrace wall and scramble onto the **Erque-Erquito** path, the zig-zagging course of which can be seen during our descent.

Bearing right, we climb gently to pass through a tunnel of broom, 20 metres after which we swing left below electricity poles (Wp.10 115M) to cross a rockspill and begin the zigzagging climb seen from above. After crossing a small spur (Wp.11 120M), the path levels out briefly then climbs to cross two more rockspills before emerging on the tip of a ridge from where we can see **Erquito** (Wp.12 135M). (Looking ESE we can see a concrete curve in the **Igualero-Playa Santiago** road. Between us and the road, there's a knoll of rock on a broad ridge defined by two watercourses. The described route climbs to the left of this ridge and is every bit as arduous as it looks!) A gentle descent (ESE) brings us onto a rocky spur, at the end of which we bear left, winding down to cross a footbridge (Wp.13 145M) onto a clear path leading to the tiny plaza of **Erquito** chapel (Wp.14 150M), where there's a charmless but functional portico offering shade and, <u>maybe</u>, water.

From the chapel, we follow the new dirt track (due to be asphalted though progress to-date has been desultory) up to the second sharp left hand bend (Wp.15 160M) just below a stone cabin, which is where the moment of truth comes. Sensible people will bear left and follow the track/lane back to the starting point, which takes about ninety minutes. The rest of us, turn right. Again, I emphasise, this is a very gruelling ascent. It has its rewards, making a perfect circular walk, avoiding the dull track/lane, and above all taking us onto the superb balcony path from **Igualero**, but it's only for the committed.

Climbing behind the cabin, in fact a roofless ruin, we ignore a broad path running SSE, and cut straight up (E) through the rocks for 50 metres to emerge on the remains of an old donkey trail (Wp.16 162M) which we follow for most of the climb. Bearing left, we follow the trail as it climbs (NE) until cairns mark a detour skirting a stretch blocked by fallen rocks and agave. Following the cairns, we cut a corner of the trail and climb towards a small, sturdy palm, after which (Wp.17 170M) we recover the paved trail and zigzag up onto a minor spur directly behind the ruined cabin (Wp.18 175M). Ignoring dirt branches to the east, we bear left (NE). From here, we can see a line of electricity pylons. The highest visible pylon is our general objective.

The trail disappears in a sheet of rock, but maintaining direction (NE), we follow cairns to a seam of yellow rock (Wp.19 185M) and bear left (NNE) on a faint path crossing tiny crumbling terraces, aiming 100 metres to the left of our guiding pylon. 50 metres before the pylon, we climb to the right of a solitary palm to rejoin the donkey trail (Wp.20 190M). Bearing right, away from the pylon, we climb a stretch of extremely rugged trail, until it dwindles to a dirt path leading to our guiding pylon (Wp.21 200M) from where we see the radio masts below **Igualero** *ermita*.

It's worth pausing to catch your breath here. Though the steepest climbing is done, the most complicated bit remains. The donkey trail traces a long detour to the north then doubles back above the rocks directly behind the pylon, but is so badly overgrown, it's simpler to climb straight over the rocks. This is not as difficult as it looks from below. Hands are required, but it's an easy scramble, comparable to the descent at Wp.5.

Following the cairn-marked route, we wind up through the lower rocks to a small bluff 30 metres east of the pylon, where we find a shelf similar to the one at Wp.5, but longer and broader. Climbing onto the bluff, we find more cairns leading to a second, much smaller outcrop of rock, behind which we recover the donkey trail (Wp.22 205M), 75 metres from the pylon. Another very steep, very rugged climb, zigzags up onto a slope below a spine of rock running along the ridge (Wp.23 210M), 150 metres from the pylon. Bearing left (NEE) we follow the trail, which is initially buried by a spill of small rocks, up to a tall cairn on the horizon (Wp.24 215M). Ignoring traces bearing right over bare rock 50 metres after the cairn, we maintain direction (NEE), on a rough, reddish brown 'way' winding through the rocks and cistus along the north-western flank of the ridge. This way curves round to the right, entering a shallow erosion channel (Wp.25 220M) on the back of the ridge, where all paths disappear!

250 metres above us is a line of wooden electricity poles. One of these poles, directly ahead of us (NE), is lined up with a metal pylon on the horizon. We join a path across the ridge between this wooden pole and its neighbour to the right. Picking our way through low cistus to a wide 'stairway' of rough, grassy terraces, we climb from terrace to terrace (NNE), keeping an eye on the two wooden poles identified from below. Towards the top, the terraces are again covered in low cistus, but tending towards the pole on the right, we find a final brief stretch of paved trail before joining a good dirt path next to a large boulder cairn (Wp.26 235M). The pathfinding problems are over!

Turning left, we follow this path over a slight rise, passing a small spring and crossing the **Igualero** watercourse. After a gentle climb, we join the waymarked path between **Igualero** and **Chipude** (Wp.27 250M). Bearing left, we follow this superb balcony path as it winds along below the pine trees with great views over the *barranco*. The path finally descends onto the **Erque** road (Wp.28 280M), 700 metres from Wp.2, 1 km from the main road.

This tiny *ermita*, so diminutive it's little more than an overgrown oratory, is perhaps the most perfectly situated on the island. Perched on a platform overlooking the **Barranco de Argaga** with fine views out to sea across the **Guerquenche** and **Mérica** ridges, it seems utterly isolated and cut off from the world, though the hamlet of **Gerián** is in fact just round the corner. Ideal for those wanting tame walking in wild country.

| 3 | 2¾-3H | 10 km | 350m ↑ 350m ↓ | ↻ | 4* |
|---|---|---|---|---|---|

*in **Cercado**

**Access**: by car and bus L1, L6 or L7. Parking is tricky in **Cercado**. If there's no room in the village, drive the start of the walk and park in the lay-by 400 metres from Wp.1.

**Strolls**
Turn left on the trail just before Wp.4 to climb into **Chipude**, returning via Walk 18 Wp.s1-5 carrying straight on at Wp.5

**Extension:** Walk 22

We leave **Cercado** on a paved lane (Wp.1 0M) opposite the new bus-stop, where the road curls round the **Barranco de la Matanza**. The paving soon gives way to tarmac, which we follow to the *colegio* on the ridge between **Cercado** and **Chipude**. Ignoring tracks to the right, we maintain direction (SE) on a donkey trail (Wp.2 10M) descending to cross a dry affluent of the **Matanza** (Wp.3 15M), after which we bear right on a dirt track. Climbing gently, we look for a blue-waymarked trail branching left, 5 metres after which, we turn right on a path (Wp.4 20M) above an immense bank of figs.

The path runs along the southern flank of the valley, passing overgrown branches to left and right. After the confluence of the **Matanza** and its affluent, the path loses its defining walls and crosses a grassy terrace then runs along a ledge below low rocks and passes a cairn-marked branch down to our return route (Wp.5 40M). Ignoring faint traces branching left 20 metres later, we stick to the main path as it winds through the rocks, crossing two faint X-

Bati following the canal.

roads, where we bear left then right, descending to join a new dirt track (Wp.6 50M). We follow the track down towards the junction of the **Matanza** and **Manantiales** ravines, which together form the **Barranco de Argaga**. At the end of the track (Wp.7 55M), we traverse a grassy terrace and, after 15 metres, turn right on a roughly cobbled path partially overgrown with bamboo. Descending onto vine terraces, where the cobbles give way to dirt, we wind down to pass in front of a small cabin, where we bear left, then right five metres later, crossing the **Manantiales** (Wp.8 65M) 100 metres above the confluence of the two *barrancos*.

We now follow a canal to the *ermita*, sometimes walking in the canal, sometimes on paths running above and below it. The way is obvious and well-marked with cairns, but if you find yourself more than 10 metres below the canal, check you haven't drifted onto one of the many minor ways descending into the valley, notably at a cairn marked branch (Wp.9 75M), where we carry straight on to rejoin the canal. At the junction with the clear, paved trail from **Valle Gran Rey** (Wp.10 78M), we ignore a branch climbing to the left and continue along the remains of the canal, until a final stretch of path climbs to the *ermita* (Wp.11 85M).

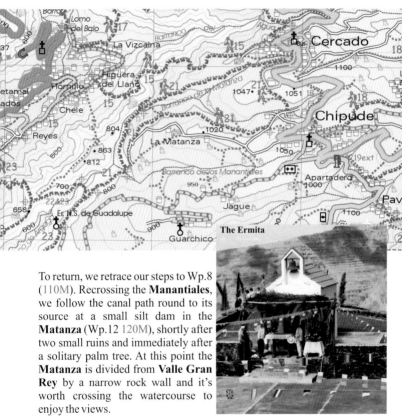

To return, we retrace our steps to Wp.8 (110M). Recrossing the **Manantiales**, we follow the canal path round to its source at a small silt dam in the **Matanza** (Wp.12 120M), shortly after two small ruins and immediately after a solitary palm tree. At this point the **Matanza** is divided from **Valle Gran Rey** by a narrow rock wall and it's worth crossing the watercourse to enjoy the views.

The Ermita

Returning to Wp.12, we continue along the left bank of the watercourse for 50 metres. Ignoring a faint path climbing to the right, we cross the watercourse and climb past a cabin-cave with a green door, bearing left at a Y-junction a few minutes later. After a steady climb, our stony path levels off before joining a section of paved trail (Wp.13 140M). Maintaining a generally easterly direction, we come to parallel dirt paths which rejoin at another paved section (Wp.14 155M). The paved trail becomes a dirt path again which, as we approach the village, dwindles to a faint trodden way for 50 metres. We then cross onto the left bank of the watercourse (Wp.15 160M), where a partially paved and cobbled trail climbs to join the *colegio* road in front of house No.12, 100 metres from Wp.1.

# 22. TEQUERGENCHE

This straightforward linear walk is a relatively easy way of seeing the **Barranco de Argaga** and also a useful preliminary excursion prior to embarking on Walk 23. The perspective on **Valle Gran Rey** from the **Tequergenche** cliffs is astonishing - perfect for those who are at once fascinated and fearful of heights! The high exertion rating is due to the rough terrain and the fact that most of the climbing is on the way back. Remember this when you're cheerfully galloping along on the outward leg. Not recommended in hot weather.

**Access**: by car. To reach the **Ermita de Nuestra Señora de Guadalupe**, take the unsignposted lane to **Chipude** cemetery, which starts at the junction of the **Cercado** and **La Dama** roads between signs for 'La Dama/La Rajita' and 'Chipude/El Cercado'. Turn right at km 4.3, in sight of **Gerián**. The *ermita* is 500 metres from the turn-off.

| | |
|---|---|
| **Short Version**: to **Las Pilas** | |
| **Extension**: Walk 21 for access by bus | |

Barranco de Argaga

Just to the right of the *ermita* (Wp.1 0M), at the end of the wall defining its small plaza, we take a narrow path heading NE above an abandoned canal. The path descends to the canal, which we follow for 25 metres before bearing left on a minor path leading down to a broader trail (Wp.2 10M) – you can also join this trail at the top, following the canal for a further 75 metres. Bearing left, we follow the trail into the **Barranco de Argaga**, ignoring a branch to the right about halfway down.

Crossing the watercourse (Wp.3 15M), we bear left through rocks, climbing onto a broad dirt path heading west along the ravine's northern flank. After a long level stretch, the path climbs slightly, passing in rapid succession three branches to the right, the first (a minor path that you may not notice) doubling back NE, the second running parallel to the main path along a terrace, the third cutting through a wide natural gateway marked by a large, faint white arrow (Wp.4 25M).

Ignoring all three turnings, we continue along the ridge to the left of two small peaks, the second of which is **Montaña Adivino**. Midway between the two peaks, a path branching right leads to a natural *mirador* overlooking **Valle Gran Rey**. Below **Adivino**, we ignore a minor fork to the left, staying on the

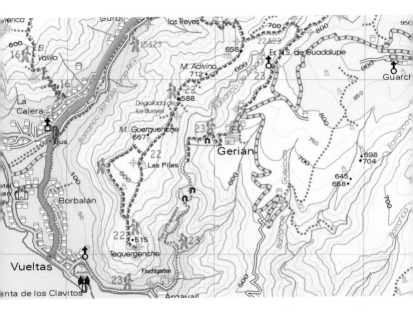

higher path, which leads to superb views down the **Barranco de Argaga** and glimpses of the beaches at the mouth of **Valle Gran Rey**. Descending toward the long narrow neck of **Degollada de los Bueyes**, we bear right at a junction with another path (Wp.5 40M) and wind down the ridge, spectacularly poised between **Valle Gran Rey** and the **Barranco de Argaga**.

Skirting to the left of a spine-like necklace of rock, we descend slightly (ignore a cairn indicating a level way along the top) through a rockier, sparser landscape where even the cactus can't get a grip and house-leeks colonise what purchase there is. We then climb to two distinct, carefully laid steps, where our route is joined by a minor path up from the *barranco*. Approaching the rise of **Montaña Guerguenche**, we pass a gateway of waist-high cairns (Wp.6 55M), where two very minor paths (one vertiginous the other verging on the suicidal) descend into **Valle Gran Rey**.

Ignoring a fork to the left 30 metres after the gateway, we resume climbing (SW), gently at first then more steadily, with fine views of the **Fortaleza** to the south-east, eventually traversing a forest of snapped agave-scapes to a ruin on top of **Guerguenche** (Wp.7 65M). Following an increasingly faint path across a stony plateau, we pass a rough threshing circle. Maintaining direction (SW) and ignoring a stone-laid way branching right, we cross rocks topped with a tall cairn, below which we descend to the **Las Pilas** ruins (Wp.8 70M) above an expanse of marginally less stony terraces.

Descending toward the distant mass of **Tequergenche**, we cross the terraces, looking for cairns indicating the way when the path, never better than obscure, virtually disappears altogether. After a steady descent, the terraces crumble into pathless scrub and we drop down to the broad saddle behind **Tequergenche**, where we can see two clear paths heading south. Taking the main, left-hand path (Wp.9 85M), we gradually bear SE to a superb natural *mirador* (Wp.10 90M) overlooking the **Barranco de Argaga**, where we can see the three palms and overhang cave passed in Walk 23.

Once we've had our fill of the views, we retrace our steps to the saddle behind **Tequergenche**, but instead of climbing back to **Las Pilas**, bear left across the reddish dirt slope, picking up a rough, cairn-marked way climbing onto the cliffs overlooking first the port at **Vueltas**, then **La Calera**, and finally the *charcos* and beaches of **Valle Gran Rey**. The views should be sufficiently impressive to discourage going too close to the cliffs.

La Calera seen from the cliffs.

Following a faint path, we climb gently between the cliffs and the tips of terraces, eventually coming onto a terrace built along the edge of the cliff and passing a sheet of corrugated iron (Wp.11 105M) weighed down with stones.

Continuing along the cliff path, largely on the level but climbing occasionally, we gradually bear NE then E, coming into view of the entire **Valle Gran Rey** and running alongside a line of young pine clinging to the cliff tops. 100 metres after the first pine, we see a large cairn on our right (Wp.12 120M), the first for some while, at which point we leave the cliff path and turn right, crossing a very broad terrace (SE then E) back to the first ruin, from where we follow our outward route back to the *ermita*.

**Note:** mountain paths never look the same in different directions. Remember to descend after the ruin, ignoring traces climbing to the crest. Likewise, stick to the main traces skirting **Adivino**. Ignore a fork to the right as you approach the gateway at Wp.4. Look out for silvery white waymarks, most of which are placed for people walking east.

# 23. BARRANCO DE ARGAGA

This is the best known and most popular 'wild' walk on La Gomera, partly because it's right next door to **Valle Gran Rey**, partly because it really is very wild, most of the climb, though well waymarked with red arrows, large dots, and cairns, being virtually pathless. Doing the route in reverse is not recommended as the waymarks are placed for people climbing. The descent into **Valle Gran Rey** is dull, but that's no bad thing after such an exciting climb. Bear in mind that references to left/right banks are the opposite of our direction. Take plenty of water. There's a standpipe at the *ermita*, but if the sun's out, the water will be hot by the time you get there! Only for experienced walkers.

**Access**: by car and bus L1 or L6. The described itinerary starts and ends at the new bus station in **La Calera** (opposite the CEPSA petrol station), but can easily be adapted if you're staying in **Valle Gran Rey**.

**Strolls**
**(a)** From **Vueltas**, continue past the mouth of the *barranco* to **Las Salinas**, the best beach on the island **(b)** on Tuesdays and Fridays, to the **Fruchtgarten**, where they claim to have planted 150 varieties of tropical or subtropical fruits.

From the bus station (Wp.1 0M), we follow the main road through **Borbalán** for a little over a kilometre, bearing left at the beach-front roundabout to the small port in **Vueltas**. Beyond the port, we take the dirt track (Wp.2 20M) that runs along the seafront below the intimidating cliffs of **Tequergenche** to the hamlet of **Argayall**, where a stout but sign-less signpost marks the mouth of the **Barranco de Argaga** (Wp.3 35M).

Following signs for the **Fruchtgarten**, we turn left on a dirt track climbing (NE) alongside the riddled walls of an old banana plantation. Ignoring a ceramic *privado* sign, we stay on the track, crossing the *barranco* watercourse three times, passing the entrance to the 'Fruit Garden' after the second crossing. Immediately after the third crossing, the track is blocked by a wire mesh fence and we drop down into the bed of the *barranco* (Wp.4 45M). Winding between boulders dotted with cairns, we pick our way upstream to a wooden footbridge where the watercourse narrows between reddish rocks. Bearing left, we climb along the rocks then drop down from a low wall and cross onto the left bank, where a path climbs above a circular reservoir built into the watercourse. After crossing or skirting (both routes are waymarked) three long terraces, we traverse the uppermost terrace, at the end of which we climb past three smaller terraces (invisible from below) interleaved with several mini-terraces. Crossing the watercourse above a silt-dam (Wp.5 60M), we follow the right bank for 75 metres before re-crossing and beginning the real climbing, very steeply, straight up a watershed.

From hereon in the majority of the climb is off-path and principally guided by old, dull red waymarks and more recent scarlet waymarks. References to 'paths' are very subjective. If you find the climbing (hands required) too much

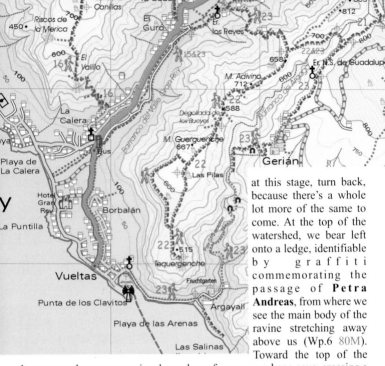

at this stage, turn back, because there's a whole lot more of the same to come. At the top of the watershed, we bear left onto a ledge, identifiable by graffiti commemorating the passage of **Petra Andreas**, from where we see the main body of the ravine stretching away above us (Wp.6 80M). Toward the top of the *barranco*, a long narrow pipe drops down from an overhang cave, crossing a spring with three palm trees. We will zigzag up below the palms, then cross the face of the cave (right to left) before climbing behind it.

At the end of a rough, mildly vertiginous path, a red arrow indicates a roughly stepped descent back into the watercourse. Ignoring a path bearing left onto terraces, we follow dots and cairns up the watercourse for 50 metres. We then climb onto terraces on the right bank before rejoining the watercourse below a cabin-cave (Wp.7 95M). Climbing back onto the left bank and crossing minute terraces and bare rock, we come to our second and most significant pathless climb. Remember, the waymarks and cairns are your best friends here. When old and new waymarks appear contradictory, follow the new ones.

After following the channel of an ancient canal, we climb onto a ledge below a small overhang cave, passing below the three palms and crossing the pipes seen from Wp.6. We then scramble past a succession of tiny caves, taking advantage of some very approximate but welcome boulder 'stairways'. After a second major boulder stairway, 'handless' walking (not a redundant comment up here) brings us across the face of the large cave seen from below (Wp.8 125M), from where we enjoy superb views back down the *barranco*. Beyond the cave, we double back on a third major boulder stairway, after which we climb straight across the rocks onto a ridge behind the cave, bringing us into view of the ravine's upper reaches.

Still relying on the waymarks, we pick our way across the rocks and follow a rough way along the left bank, passing a precipitous drop and crossing a boulder strewn gully before descending onto a terrace, at the end of which we see a palm and a pipe (Wp.9 140M). We are now in the wildest most isolated corner of the ravine and the silence is total. Skirting a narrow ledge at the end of the terrace, we double back just before the palm on more boulder 'stairs'. After crossing more rocks, we bear right on a very steep but distinct stone path climbing alongside terraces (Wp.10 145M).

After 50 metres, we traverse a terrace to the left before resuming our steep climb on a rough, dirt, gravel, and rock path. The path levels off briefly before climbing on an easier gradient to cross the smooth rocks of a watershed, 50 metres after which we veer right, climbing steadily then steeply up a spur alongside the watershed. Ignoring all branches, we pass a walled in cave (Wp.11 170M) and cross the head of the watershed. Still climbing, we curve round to the right of and then through rocks speckled with the letter 'M' to a 'Parque Rural Valle Gran Rey' signpost (Wp.12 190M) just below the hamlet of **Gerián**, which is invisible till the last moment.

**Barranco de Argaga**

Following the tarmac lane through the hamlet, we pass a small shrine, 30 metres after which, we branch left on a broad path (Wp.13 195M) marked with a metal spike with a nut on its tip. Climbing <u>between</u> two houses, we bear north <u>behind</u> the smaller house on the left onto a broad trail from where we can see the tiny **Ermita de Nuestra Señora de Guadalupe**. When the trail bears right, back towards the lane, we branch left on a dirt path running along a terrace to the *ermita* (Wp.14 205M).

From the *ermita*, we follow the canal path down to a donkey trail (Wp.15 210M) descending to cross the **Barranco de Argaga** watercourse (Wp.16 215M) before climbing (W) to a wide rock gateway marked with a large but faint white arrow (Wp.17 230M) (See Walk 22 Wps.1-4 for details).

Leaving the main path as it continues toward **Tequergenche**, we bear right, going through the gateway onto a clear path heading initially NNE, from where we can see the white walls and orange roof of **Ermita los Reyes**, way below us at the bottom of a broad watercourse. The path gradually bears NW, winding down a narrow rocky ridge to pass a scattered stand of palm below a ramshackle cabin given over to goats (Wp.18 245M). We then climb very slightly round the nose of the ridge, away from the *ermita* (NEE), after which a series of tight zigzags descend a secondary spur to a junction (Wp.19 255M). The main trail bears right, but both routes rejoin further down the spur, for a final cobbled descent to two small houses, where we join the path (Wp.20 265M) to **La Calera**, five minutes from the *ermita*, thirty minutes from the bus-station (See Walk 15 Wp.8+ for details).

# 24. BARRANCO DE ARURE

On the whole, water is altogether too precious a commodity in the Canaries to be allowed to do anything so wasteful as falling and there are only two streams on La Gomera (the **Barrancos del Cedro** and **de Arure**) that aren't siphoned off at source. In this itinerary we follow the **Arure** stream to the prettiest waterfall on the island. It's a popular walk, largely because it gives a sense of adventure without actually being alarmingly adventurous, so don't be surprised if you meet a large party of elderly German hikers just when you thought you were really getting off the beaten track. For all its popularity though, the deeper we go into the ravine, the more real the adventure seems. Ideal in hot weather. Beware of slippery rocks, especially on the return.

| | | **Stroll** |
|---|---|---|
| **Access**: by car and bus 🚌 L1 or L6 | | Circuit round **Guro**, bearing right at the tin plaques |

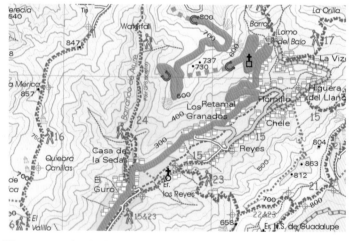

We start opposite the long roadside car-park between **Guro** and **Casa de la Seda**, 50 metres east of the phone booth and 'Los Enanitos' nursery school, where somebody has helpfully painted 'Wasserfall' on a tall palm tree (Wp.1 0M). Following a broad, paved pathway, we cross the watercourse then climb steadily through **Guro**, turning right at a junction marked with yellow-and-green arrows and another 'wasserfall' sign. The paved way soon runs into a dirt path and leaves the village, joining a canal path amid a flurry of waymarks (Wp.2 10M).

We follow the canal for 75 metres till another embarrassment of waymarks indicates where we branch left, climbing across terraces of agave and cactus spurge on a route waymarked to such surreal excess it's almost decorated. Dropping down to descend a rough gully, we cross the watercourse onto the left bank, at which point, just when they might have been useful, the waymarks disappear! Bearing left along a terrace below two tin plaques hanging from a retaining wall, we rejoin the watercourse (now a flowing stream) 75 metres later next to a length of corroded black pipe (Wp.3 20M).

Either crossing the stream and climbing a small rise or walking directly upstream (both routes rejoin), we weave in and out of the water, following occasional cairns. Emerging from a corridor of bamboo, we climb to the left of the first of four mini-waterfalls. Skirting to the right of a second mini-fall 50 metres later, we climb across a long sheet of rock and, 75 metres after that, bear left (Wp.4 35M) climbing across terraces (hands required) dotted with cairns and old red waymarks.

A narrow path tunnels through brambles before rejoining the stream, 50 metres along which we ignore a large red arrow (Wp.5 40M) apparently suggesting we take up rock-climbing. Instead, we follow a faint path along the left bank, dipping into, out of, then back into the stream, and passing the figure of a man painted on the rock. We now simply follow the stream, skirting two more mini-falls before running into, almost literally, the main waterfall (50M).

The main waterfall

Retracing our route to the first crossing of the watercourse (80M), we bear left after the tin plaques, passing graffiti scoured prickly pear and climbing behind a small sheepfold onto a canal path. The canal path is overgrown after 25 metres and we have to drop down beyond the sheepfold before climbing to cross a terrace and rejoin the canal. Stepping over a collapsing chicken-wire fence, we follow the canal for another 25 metres before bearing right, descending on a rough path toward orchards, just above which we climb slightly before joining a paved path leading to the road, 50 metres from our starting point.

Elsewhere in this book, we talk about paths being 'improbable' or 'impossible', but the two routes between **Taguluche** and the **Mirador de Arure** simply beggar belief. And why they needed <u>two</u> of them, is anybody's guess! One thing is for certain, you had to be very hungry or very frightened to contemplate beating a path up here. Nowadays all you need is a desire to experience one of the most remarkable walks on the entire island. It doesn't make any more sense than it ever did, but it's tremendous fun. At first glance, using the steepest route for the descent may seem bizarre, but there are sound reasons for this. First, the path down is so obscure in places, it's doubtful you'd find it going up. Secondly, if you did, it looks so daunting from below, you'd probably give up long before the top. Doing it as a descent, you can comfort yourself with the knowledge that things get better rather than worse! Only for experienced walkers with a good head for heights. If uncertain, visit the *mirador* first and check the start of the descent to see how you feel about it.

**Access**: by car and bus (from Wp.7) L1 or L6 (see Walk 16). Motorists park 6 km after the **Taguluche** turn-off, at the half-built (liable to remain that way) bottling plant, a large cement superstructure with maroon panels, just past a 'headless pedestrian' road sign.

**Stroll**
Fom **Arure** to the *mirador* and on to Wp.6 (see Walk 16). Follow the route of the ascent in reverse for five minutes; the views are every bit as dramatic as those from the *mirador*.

**Short Version**
Taxi to **Taguluche** and do the ascent

50 metres west of the bottling plant (Wp.1 0M), we leave the road and fork left on a tarmac track climbing toward houses. Ignoring a branch to the left, we take a concrete ramp descending in front of two modern houses onto a terrace path. Passing above one small and between two large reservoirs, we bear left on a path climbing from the village (Wp.2 5M). Ignoring a paved branch climbing to the upper reservoir, we follow a cairn-marked dirt path (SE) to a second paved trail. The trail climbs steadily alongside grassy terraces dotted with splashes of pale blue paint demarcating a property boundary to a *Monumento Natural* signpost for 'Lomo del Carretón' (Wp.3 15M).

Ignoring all branch paths, we climb steadily, coming into view of an orange cliff (SW) below pine trees, the start of our final ascent. Bearing right above a broad watercourse and passing reeds concealing a spring (Wp.4 35M), we head for the orange cliffs on an easier gradient. After traversing several watersheds and a long, sloping sheet of rock, we pass a line of three pines at the lower end of the hanger (Wp.5 45M) and cross a spill of rubble, from where the retaining walls of the

**Enjoying the views *en route*.**

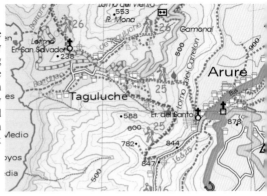

path through the woods are clearly visible. Zigzagging steeply up through the woods, we go through a natural rock gateway before winding round across bare rock to join the **Mérica** dirt track (Wp.6 70M).

Bearing left, we follow the dirt track onto the tarmac lane to **Arure**. 100 metres after the start of the tarmac, we double back to the left on a paved trail leading to the **Mirador de Arure**. Crossing the *mirador* and passing the **Ermita del Santo**, we come to a vertiginous path heading north, 30 metres along which we reach a Y-junction (Wp.7 85M). The main branch straight ahead eventually descends to Wp.15 of Walk 26, but we bear left to begin our precipitous descent. Given that the descent is a bit 'delicate', timings are even more subjective than usual. If it's of any comfort, look back from here at the orange cliff passed on the way up: from this perspective, there's clearly no way up there either!

Our path descends a long broad sloping ledge to a small stand of pine, where it narrows as it traverses a low cliff onto the first and most vertiginous of several steeply raked 'stairways'. After picking our way down the steps with considerable circumspection (handholds comforting but not compulsory), we come to a long, more or less level path, below low cliffs - again care required.

After 150 metres, another 'stairway' doubles back onto a painstaking but not manifestly dangerous way zigzagging down across a shallow rocky spur overlooking…well, just about everything (!), at the bottom of which we come to an area of scrub, rock and loose scree next to a wooden electricity post (Wp.8 110M). Two more stairways bring us down to a cement clad, piped spring (Wp.9 115M) next to a small stand of willow clustered round a solitary laurel. Crossing the main pipe and a narrower one just afterwards, we have a short but very steep, very skittery descent on very loose dirt (hands and bottom required!), before passing back under the power cable onto an abandoned terrace (Wp.10 120M).

Bearing right, we follow a very narrow path winding between a small jungle of shrubs, bushes and saplings before crossing another pipe and passing below a tiny ruin (Wp.11 125M), where the path finally clears. Winding down steeply, though nothing compared to what we've done already, we descend a long, narrow spur, following the line of the electricity cable. Joining a more substantial path (Wp.12 135M), we bear right, passing a new stone house, from where we have a straightforward descent to join the branch tarmac track ignored at the start of the walk (Wp.13 145M), 100 metres from our outward route. If descending from the **Arure** bus-stop, bear left at the T-junction 100 metres down this lane to pick up the start of the walk.

Despite its wild appearance, La Gomera has been thoroughly domesticated by centuries of back breaking labour, but there are some corners that were never properly tamed, notably the rocky landscape between **Taguluche** and **Alojera**. The **Barranco de Guarañet** (aka **Guariñen**) was never really up for domestication and, apart from a handful of forlorn-looking terraces, man seems to have been quick to concede this, leaving the land to itself and whatever a few unfastidious goats could extract from it. There's a corresponding lack of paths, but that's all to the good in one the wildest walks on the island. Not recommended after (or during!) heavy rain. The extension is only for sure-footed, confident walkers, as it's virtually pathless, very rough, and requires a knack for identifying cairns in a landscape dappled with random piles of rock.

| 5 | 3H * | 10 km | | 500m 500m | | 0 |

\* + 1 hour for the extension

**Access**: by car. Park under the flamboyant tree (Caesalpinia pulcherrima) on the left of the *ermita* parking area. You'll be glad of the shade at the end of the day.

**Short Version**: Tejeleche (see text)

**Extension**: Tejeleche (see text)

Crossing the plaza in front of the **Ermita de San Salvador** (Wp.1 0M), we take the path to the right between flamboyants and oleander. The path is rough and narrow but reasonably clear as it meanders across the slope below **Lomo del Viento** towards a large empty reservoir. Crossing a succession of watershed channels, we pass above the reservoir (Wp.2 5M), immediately after which, we ignore a cairn-marked branch climbing to the right and stick to the slightly clearer path, descending to cross a shallow gully and the nose of a small bare spur. The path becomes narrower and more badly eroded as it crosses a succession of small watersheds and minor gullies before a spill of neat terraces lead us into the bed of the *barranco* (Wp.3 20M).

In the *barranco*.

Climbing up the watercourse, we cross a remarkable variety of rocks, striated with a web of mineral salts and speckled with the thread-like fossils of tiny lichen roots. We then scramble over a series of rock chutes, passing several muddy watering holes. Drawing abreast of the first affluent watershed on the left, we come to what is effectively a Y-junction (Wp.4 35M), where we bear left, soon coming into view of dentate crash barriers on the road above us. The two branches of the streambed soon rejoin and we continue our climb, skirting huge boulders naturally cemented to the rock. Branching left at each fork in the streambed, we come to a series of cairns

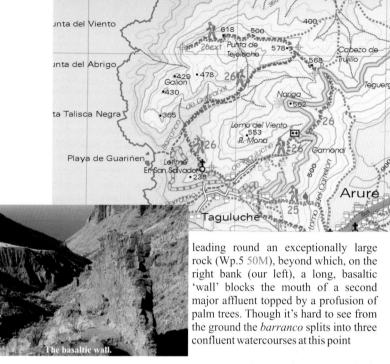

The basaltic wall.

leading round an exceptionally large rock (Wp.5 50M), beyond which, on the right bank (our left), a long, basaltic 'wall' blocks the mouth of a second major affluent topped by a profusion of palm trees. Though it's hard to see from the ground the *barranco* splits into three confluent watercourses at this point

75 metres after the large rock we leave the bed of the stream, turning left on a 'way' marked by large cairns, climbing alongside the basaltic wall toward a natural gateway gouged by water from the affluent. Crossing a ledge between the gateway and a low, dry waterfall (Wp.6 55M) we join a rough but reasonably clear goat path. Climbing steeply along the ridge between the confluent watercourses, we follow the wall, which is fascinatingly fissured with a mosaic-like craquelure, up to what looks like a blunt outcrop of rock (Wp.7 70M) but is in fact a distinct spine along the narrowest part of the ridge, providing enough shade in the morning to make a convenient rest stop.

Resuming our ascent, we cross the remains of an old retaining wall and climb to a point, 30 metres below a square mouthed cave, where the way is apparently blocked by a large pile of rocks (Wp.8 80M). Climbing over the pile of rocks, we come to a less strenuous ascent (E) below small crags flanking the ravine, crossing what appears to be another, lower basaltic wall (Wp.9 95M) but is actually a continuation of the previous wall, after which a final zigzagging ascent brings us onto the **Tejeleche** ridge (Wp.10 105M) from where we can see **Alojera** to the north.

**Short Version and Extension**
To reach Wp.10 for the short version, take the path west from the U-bend lay-by 3 km from the **Taguluche** turn-off (Wp.14), also identifiable by a wooden *Monumento Natural* post on the left just before the U-bend. If adding the extension to the main walk, turn left at Wp.10. Bear in mind that mountains never look the same in different directions, so memorise key points en route. To begin with the path is narrow and eroded, but at least obvious, as it skirts the northern side of the ridge. It then virtually disappears as we descend slightly below two palm trees and pass between two more (the second of

which is invisible at first, so it seems as if we're passing below three palm trees). After the palm trees, the path becomes clearer again, passing a branch climbing from Alojera (Wp.11 5M from Wp.10), a few minutes after which we cross a pass onto the southern side of the ridge, from where we can see the road to **Playa Guariñen**. Winding along the ridge, we cross a grassy (by local standards) saddle overlooking **Playa Alojera** (Wp.12 10M). Ignoring traces descending to the left, we climb a faint partially cairned route, crossing the head of the affluent that debouches at Wp.6. Following the cairns, we climb to the left of the highest peak on the **Tejeleche** ridge, after which we pass below a peak crowned with a diminutive square cave, coming into view of the **Ermita de San Salvador**. Continuing alongside seams of red, yellow and even mauve rock, we see the **Galión**, which is impressive, but requires a remarkably vivid imagination if we're to conjure anything galleon-like out of it. We then make for a final, tall cairn, where we bear right and climb to the last slightly vertiginous peak on the ridge (Wp.13 30M).

**To continue the main walk from WP10**
We bear right (SE) dipping down briefly on a clear path before climbing a small rise and joining the road at a lay-by on a U-bend (Wp.14 110M excluding extension). Bearing left for 30 metres to the concrete crash barriers, we ignore a path on the left down to **Alojera** and turn right on a broad path climbing a shelf of rock, marked by a vandalised *Monumento Natural* sign for **Lomo del Carretón** (the name plate may have disappeared, but the sturdy post should be there). After the stiff climb up the ravine, this may seem like a striking piece of lunacy only to be recommended to the strictly witless, especially since we soon rejoin the road, but it cuts off a long bruisingly hot detour on the road, so the extra climb is worth it.

The path climbs onto the *lomo* and approaches a small electricity pylon, 50 metres before which, we bear right at a Y-junction (Wp.15 115M). The path then runs parallel to the road passing between palm trees, which are a bit weary but provide adequate shade for a picnic on a hot day. Ignoring a clear path branching right to another pylon, we bear left (Wp.16 120M) on a broad, rough, cairn-marked way, at the end of which we recover the path. After crossing one of the gullies feeding into the **Barranco de Taguluche**, the path becomes very narrow as it winds between increasingly intrusive agave and wax plant before dropping, almost literally, onto the road at another lay-by-bend above the cemetery (Wp.17 135M). Bearing left, we follow the road for 100 metres then double back on an asphalted track down to the cemetery, at the gates of which we turn left towards another pylon on a rough, initially litter strewn path that then zigzags down to the main watercourse of the *barranco* (Wp.18 150M), where we have a choice of routes.

The simplest and most enjoyable thing to do is turn right and follow the bed of the watercourse, walking in or alongside it as convenient. There's no path and some care is called for on slippery damp patches, but after a steady, straightforward ten minute descent, we come to a final permanently slippery stretch just above a small reservoir, beyond which we join the road. Alternatively, if you've had enough rock-hopping for one day or the *barranco* is too wet, cross both the watercourse and, 50 metres later, a rough affluent, from where a clear path cuts across well-maintained terraces to pass above a small abandoned house. Bearing left, we join a dirt track leading to the road. Either way, we then follow the road back to the **Ermita de San Salvador**.

**See the notes on GPS use and waypoints on page 18.**

### 13. ARURE - LAS HAYAS

| Wp | N | W |
|---|---|---|
| 1 | 28 08.1246 | 17 19.0818 |
| 2 | 28 08.0112 | 17 19.0554 |
| 3 | 28 08.1804 | 17 18.7200 |
| 4 | 28 08.4246 | 17 18.3846 |
| 5 | 28 08.3202 | 17 18.2334 |
| 6 | 28 08.1390 | 17 17.9772 |
| 7 | 28 07.8144 | 17 17.5728 |
| 8 | 28 07.8168 | 17 17.3766 |
| 9 | 28 08.0364 | 17 17.3904 |
| 10 | 28 08.1348 | 17 17.3574 |
| 11 | 28 08.3502 | 17 17.4882 |
| 12 | 28 08.4348 | 17 17.3952 |
| 13 | 28 08.3472 | 17 17.0508 |
| 14 | 28 08.5842 | 17 17.1444 |
| 15 | 28 08.8638 | 17 17.4642 |
| 16 | 28 08.6016 | 17 17.7816 |
| 17 | 28 08.5170 | 17 18.2082 |
| 18 | 28 08.4018 | 17 18.6342 |
| 19 | 28 08.3796 | 17 18.7992 |

### 14. LAS CRECES: ROUNDABOUT ROUTE

| Wp | N | W |
|---|---|---|
| 1 | 28 07.7286 | 17 17.5050 |
| 2 | 28 07.5666 | 17 17.5140 |
| 3 | 28 07.4004 | 17 17.3958 |
| 4 | 28 07.3758 | 17 17.2674 |
| 5 | 28 07.2576 | 17 17.1534 |
| 6 | 28 07.1526 | 17 17.2002 |
| 7 | 28 07.3062 | 17 16.8042 |
| 8 | 28 07.6410 | 17 16.8588 |
| 9 | 28 07.7748 | 17 16.9500 |
| 10 | 28 07.9116 | 17 16.5876 |
| 11 | 28 08.5812 | 17 17.1204 |
| 12 | 28 08.3412 | 17 17.0526 |
| 13 | 28 08.0365 | 17 17.3905 |
| 14 | 28 07.8108 | 17 17.3814 |

### 15. CERCADO - VALLE GRAN REY

| Wp | N | W |
|---|---|---|
| 1 | 28 07.1454 | 17 17.2056 |
| 2 | 28 07.0620 | 17 17.4432 |
| 3 | 28 07.0170 | 17 17.7738 |
| 4 | 28 06.9690 | 17 17.9844 |
| 5 | 28 06.8334 | 17 18.3108 |
| 6 | 28 06.9342 | 17 18.3990 |
| 7 | 28 06.6318 | 17 18.9072 |
| 8 | 28 06.5244 | 17 19.0470 |
| 9 | 28 06.3840 | 17 19.3716 |
| 10 | 28 06.3720 | 17 19.4820 |
| 11 | 28 05.6286 | 17 20.1126 |

### 16. LA MÉRICA

| Wp | N | W |
|---|---|---|
| 1 | 28 08.1288 | 17 19.0854 |
| 2 | 28 07.7190 | 17 19.6488 |
| 3 | 28 07.3878 | 17 19.7376 |
| 4 | 28 06.9324 | 17 20.1354 |
| 5 | 28 06.4428 | 17 20.1840 |
| 6 | 28 06.2778 | 17 20.2644 |
| 7 | 28 06.0480 | 17 20.2392 |
| 8 | 28 05.9712 | 17 20.1168 |
| 9 | 28 05.8836 | 17 19.9854 |
| 10 | 28 05.7090 | 17 20.1042 |

### 17. VALLE GRAN REY - HAYAS

| Wp | N | W |
|---|---|---|
| 1 | 28 07.2270 | 17 18.5826 |
| 2 | 28 07.3482 | 17 18.6108 |
| 3 | 28 07.3794 | 17 18.6336 |
| 4 | 28 07.3734 | 17 18.6720 |
| 5 | 28 07.4796 | 17 18.5358 |
| 6 | 28 07.5084 | 17 18.5520 |
| 7 | 28 07.6230 | 17 18.3804 |
| 8 | 28 07.6524 | 17 18.0744 |
| 9 | 28 07.7718 | 17 17.5530 |
| 10 | 28 07.5324 | 17 17.4942 |
| 11 | 28 07.4250 | 17 17.6904 |
| 12 | 28 07.3848 | 17 17.9046 |
| 13 | 28 07.2858 | 17 18.2442 |
| 14 | 28 07.1268 | 17 18.3276 |

### 18. CHIPUDE - GARAJONAY

| Wp | N | W |
|---|---|---|
| 1 | 28 06.5910 | 17 16.8846 |
| 2 | 28 06.7164 | 17 16.9638 |
| 3 | 28 06.7992 | 17 16.8924 |
| 4 | 28 06.9222 | 17 16.9296 |
| 5 | 28 06.9540 | 17 17.0226 |
| 6 | 28 07.1004 | 17 16.6416 |
| 7 | 28 07.0398 | 17 16.2282 |
| 8 | 28 06.9888 | 17 15.8922 |
| 9 | 28 06.9906 | 17 15.6504 |
| 10 | 28 06.8706 | 17 15.5400 |
| 11 | 28 06.7482 | 17 15.0858 |
| 12 | 28 06.6816 | 17 14.8386 |
| 13 | 28 06.2616 | 17 14.8566 |
| 14 | 28 06.6330 | 17 14.7654 |
| 15 | 28 06.5868 | 17 14.9016 |
| 16 | 28 06.6792 | 17 14.7600 |
| 17 | 28 06.8568 | 17 15.7506 |
| 18 | 28 06.8658 | 17 16.3350 |
| 19 | 28 06.8178 | 17 16.3494 |
| 20 | 28 06.7788 | 17 16.6266 |
| 21 | 28 06.6348 | 17 16.7592 |

### 19. FORTALEZA

| Wp | N | W |
|---|---|---|
| 1 | 28 06.4602 | 17 16.0566 |
| 2 | 28 06.3702 | 17 16.1070 |
| 3 | 28 06.4464 | 17 16.2426 |
| 4 | 28 06.3858 | 17 16.5918 |
| 5 | 28 06.2994 | 17 16.5270 |
| 6 | 28 06.2376 | 17 16.5228 |
| 7 | 28 06.1410 | 17 16.3878 |
| 8 | 28 06.0984 | 17 16.4718 |
| 9 | 28 06.0708 | 17 16.5168 |
| 10 | 28 06.0546 | 17 16.5630 |
| 11 | 28 05.9388 | 17 16.6548 |
| 12 | 28 06.5016 | 17 16.7790 |

## 20.
### BARRANCO DE ERQUE

| Wp | N | W |
|---|---|---|
| 1 | 28 06.4596 | 17 16.0524 |
| 2 | 28 06.3306 | 17 16.1412 |
| 3 | 28 06.1362 | 17 16.3728 |
| 4 | 28 06.1200 | 17 16.4124 |
| 5 | 28 06.0984 | 17 16.3392 |
| 6 | 28 06.0450 | 17 16.2516 |
| 7 | 28 05.9292 | 17 16.2150 |
| 8 | 28 05.7822 | 17 16.1532 |
| 9 | 28 05.7996 | 17 16.0506 |
| 10 | 28 05.6994 | 17 16.0656 |
| 11 | 28 05.6430 | 17 16.0824 |
| 12 | 28 05.5008 | 17 16.0638 |
| 13 | 28 05.4096 | 17 15.9462 |
| 14 | 28 05.2872 | 17 15.9738 |
| 15 | 28 05.2428 | 17 15.8934 |
| 16 | 28 05.2272 | 17 15.8688 |
| 17 | 28 05.2716 | 17 15.8160 |
| 18 | 28 05.2518 | 17 15.7800 |
| 19 | 28 05.3262 | 17 15.6942 |
| 20 | 28 05.3916 | 17 15.6762 |
| 21 | 28 05.4234 | 17 15.6642 |
| 22 | 28 05.4126 | 17 15.6222 |
| 23 | 28 05.3886 | 17 15.5904 |
| 24 | 28 05.4018 | 17 15.5418 |
| 25 | 28 05.4546 | 17 15.4542 |
| 26 | 28 05.5440 | 17 15.3192 |
| 27 | 28 05.8326 | 17 15.3870 |
| 28 | 28 06.4971 | 17 15.8283 |

## 21.
### ERMITA DE NUESTRA SEÑORA DE GUADALUPE

| Wp | N | W |
|---|---|---|
| 1 | 28 07.1250 | 17 17.0550 |
| 2 | 28 06.8586 | 17 17.2098 |
| 3 | 28 06.7482 | 17 17.0976 |
| 4 | 28 06.6408 | 17 17.2428 |
| 5 | 28 06.7170 | 17 17.9262 |
| 6 | 28 06.5760 | 17 18.1314 |
| 7 | 28 06.4626 | 17 18.1500 |
| 8 | 28 06.3972 | 17 18.1920 |
| 9 | 28 06.2820 | 17 18.4134 |
| 10 | 28 06.2100 | 17 18.4788 |
| 11 | 28 06.0882 | 17 18.6210 |
| 12 | 28 06.7548 | 17 18.1152 |
| 13 | 28 06.9228 | 17 17.6346 |
| 14 | 28 06.9432 | 17 17.5134 |
| 15 | 28 07.0176 | 17 17.3388 |

## 22.
### TEQUERGENCHE

| Wp | N | W |
|---|---|---|
| 1 | 28 06.0900 | 17 18.6222 |
| 2 | 28 06.2328 | 17 18.4686 |
| 3 | 28 06.3294 | 17 18.5034 |
| 4 | 28 06.2196 | 17 18.8208 |
| 5 | 28 05.9856 | 17 19.1508 |
| 6 | 28 05.7918 | 17 19.3176 |
| 7 | 28 05.6262 | 17 19.4376 |
| 8 | 28 05.4960 | 17 19.5102 |
| 9 | 28 05.1870 | 17 19.6026 |
| 10 | 28 05.0310 | 17 19.5336 |
| 11 | 28 05.3658 | 17 19.6308 |
| 12 | 28 05.6490 | 17 19.5390 |

## 23.
### BARRANCO DE ARGAGA

| Wp | N | W |
|---|---|---|
| 1 | 28 05.6088 | 17 20.1174 |
| 2 | 28 04.9602 | 17 19.9194 |
| 3 | 28 04.8216 | 17 19.4466 |
| 4 | 28 04.9206 | 17 19.2696 |
| 5 | 28 05.1036 | 17 19.3374 |
| 6 | 28 05.2110 | 17 19.2756 |
| 7 | 28 05.2968 | 17 19.2162 |
| 8 | 28 05.3760 | 17 19.1796 |
| 9 | 28 05.4762 | 17 19.2204 |
| 10 | 28 05.5146 | 17 19.2246 |
| 11 | 28 05.6754 | 17 19.0638 |
| 12 | 28 05.7054 | 17 18.9552 |
| 13 | 28 05.7864 | 17 18.8532 |
| 14 | 28 06.0810 | 17 18.6192 |
| 15 | 28 06.2346 | 17 18.4686 |
| 16 | 28 06.3294 | 17 18.5040 |
| 17 | 28 06.2208 | 17 18.8334 |
| 18 | 28 06.3300 | 17 18.9954 |
| 19 | 28 06.4404 | 17 19.0686 |
| 20 | 28 06.4938 | 17 19.2450 |

## 24.
### BARRANCO DE ARURE

| Wp | N | W |
|---|---|---|
| 1 | 28 06.4590 | 17 19.5606 |
| 2 | 28 06.5058 | 17 19.6038 |
| 3 | 28 06.6990 | 17 19.5606 |
| 4 | 28 06.9084 | 17 19.4874 |
| 5 | 28 07.0050 | 17 19.5024 |

## 25.
### LOMO DE CARRETÓN

| Wp | N | W |
|---|---|---|
| 1 | 28 08.2398 | 17 19.7724 |
| 2 | 28 08.0958 | 17 19.8324 |
| 3 | 28 08.0526 | 17 19.6986 |
| 4 | 28 07.9752 | 17 19.5498 |
| 5 | 28 07.8330 | 17 19.6140 |
| 6 | 28 07.7220 | 17 19.6488 |
| 7 | 28 07.9914 | 17 19.4058 |
| 8 | 28 08.1222 | 17 19.4658 |
| 9 | 28 08.1498 | 17 19.5078 |
| 10 | 28 08.1342 | 17 19.5378 |
| 11 | 28 08.1486 | 17 19.5678 |
| 12 | 28 08.1660 | 17 19.6620 |
| 13 | 28 08.1912 | 17 19.7868 |

## 26.
### BARRANCO DE GUARAÑET

| Wp | N | W |
|---|---|---|
| 1 | 28 08.3214 | 17 20.2434 |
| 2 | 28 08.4264 | 17 20.2956 |
| 3 | 28 08.6214 | 17 20.3490 |
| 4 | 28 08.7030 | 17 20.2254 |
| 5 | 28 08.7348 | 17 20.0778 |
| 6 | 28 08.7690 | 17 20.0172 |
| 7 | 28 08.8182 | 17 19.9422 |
| 8 | 28 08.8956 | 17 19.8786 |
| 9 | 28 08.9562 | 17 19.6620 |
| 10 | 28 08.9994 | 17 19.6056 |
| 11 | 28 09.0912 | 17 19.7136 |
| 12 | 28 09.1128 | 17 19.9230 |
| 13 | 28 09.0438 | 17 20.3478 |
| 14 | 28 08.9112 | 17 19.4454 |
| 15 | 28 08.8338 | 17 19.3770 |
| 16 | 28 08.6940 | 17 19.4652 |
| 17 | 28 08.5554 | 17 19.5696 |
| 18 | 28 08.4336 | 17 19.6440 |

**Tunel de la Cumbre** is **San Sebastian's** 'gate' to the North. Emerging from the old tunnel, we plunge down into the **Hermigua** valley, the road thankfully much improved and with wooden crash barriers while the landscape is noticeable more orogenical than during the climb up from the capital. Behind the mountains on our left is the hidden valley of **El Cedro**, as we sweep down to the first settlements. Agriculture is still important in this region, with more terraces in cultivation than other regions of **La Gomera**. **Hermigua** and **Vallehermoso** were once the power houses of the Gomeran economy, quays being built on the sea-fronts to load the abundant agricultural products directly onto ships. It is not so important now but the remains of the quays are still there and the old days are remembered in sepia photographs on bar walls.

Old houses line the main road around **Hermigua**'s 16th century church while small settlements line the valley. Walkways and narrow roads link the town and settlements, making for easy strolling around the valley as an alternative to our more strenuous official routes. Running out of the valley our road returns to a dramatic cliff face setting before crossing the bridge to **Agulo**, one of La Gomera's most photographed settlements due to its dramatic backdrop against **Mount Teide** on Tenerife. Across the road, dramatic cliffs climb up to the **Palmita** valley; Walk 32 takes us up that impossible looking cliff face (but only in good weather). **Agulo**'s quiet streets provide another opportunity for easy strolling as a respite from the steep landscape.

A tunnel and a cliff-side drive, again thankfully improved, bring us to **Las Rosas**; turn left here to climb up to the **Centro de Visitantes** information centre, or follow the narrow road out past the *embalse* to the highly regarded **Bodegon Roque Blanco** bar/restaurant with *mirador* views from its terrace (Walk 29). Passing through **Las Rosas**, the landscape seems quite gentle until we swing west to overlook the dramatic northern valleys containing the **Simancasa** and **Tamagarda** settlements, even the main road seeming vertiginous in places. If this isn't dramatic enough, emerging from the next tunnel into the massive **Vallehermoso** valley cannot fail to impress. **Roque Cano** might not be the highest peak on the island, but it dominates the town and valley with its massive presence.

A proliferation of fine old houses give **Vallehermoso** a prestigious air despite the newer developments. Cultivators and trailers, a popular work/utility local form of transport cluster around the bars along with modern four wheel drives; almost everybody seeming to drive something vaguely agricultural in this most traditional of towns. Gaze up the western valley wall - yes, it is terraced to its very top, though now only the lower terraces are cultivated. From town the narrow 'main' road climbs up past the higher settlements before a tortuous ascent brings us up to the spectacularly sited tourist bar/restaurants at **Chorros de Epina**. Even these comparatively modern businesses retaining a traditional air reminiscent of the previous millennium.

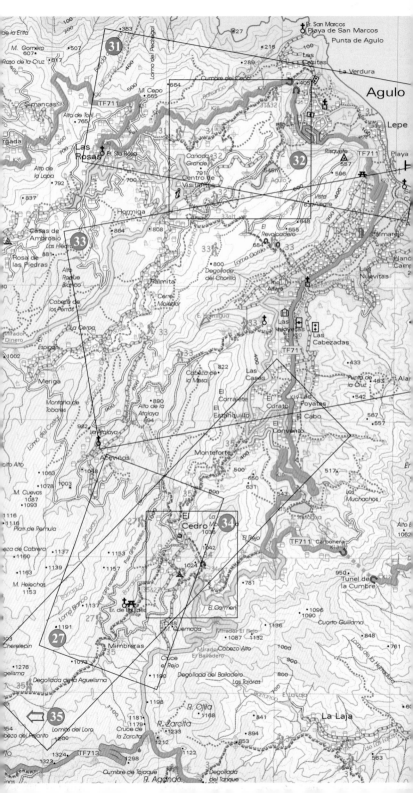

# 27. LAS MIMBRERAS

For motorists disinclined to tackle the rigorous descent of Walk 35 or the claustrophobia of Walk 34, this short circuit is an ideal ramble through the heart of the **Garajonay**. *Mimbrera* is Spanish for crack willow or osier. In common with other willows, the Canary willow (*Salix canariensis*) contains salicylic acid and was traditionally used as an analgesic.

| | | | | | | |
|---|---|---|---|---|---|---|
| 3 | 1H 20M | 4.5 km | | ↗ 200m ↘ 200m | ↻ | 4 |

> **Stroll**
> From **Las Mimbreras** parking area, take the **El Contadero** path (S). When the signposted route branches left, stay on the main trail, curving through a gentle climb before rejoining the signposted route. Bearing left for **Arroyo de El Cedro**, cross the stream and follow the right bank till a bridge leads back to the **Mimbreras** path.
>
> **Extension**: Walk 34

**Access**: by car

Leaving our vehicle at the **Mimbreras** parking area (Wp.1 0M), we continue along the dirt track (NNE), immediately passing a series of mini 'caves', in fact barbecue pits once used by forestry workers. After a gentle twenty-minute climb, the track levels out and we glimpse **Hermigua**, the **Barranco del Cedro** and the sea, through trees so heavily rimed with lichen it hangs like hanks of fur. Shortly before a branch track to the right, we leave the main track, turning right on a path signposted 'Caserio de El Cedro' 1.3 (Wp.2 35M).

At a Y-junction 30 metres later, our path branches right, but it's worth bearing left for a few metres to a natural *mirador* overlooking the *barrancos* behind **Agulo**. Descending between banks of the colonising 'Cats Ear' creeper (Tradescantia fluminensis), we turn right at a junction next to a minor dirt track and continue through woods so tangled and be-lichened they resemble a fairytale landscape. A steady zigzagging descent leads to another natural *mirador*, after which we come to a stripped hillside above a military green bungalow. Crossing a dusty dirt track leading to the **La Vista Casa Rural** (Wp.3 50M), we bear right on a slithery dirt path traversing a terrace below the *casa rural* and descend along a ridge between terraces. Towards the end of the ridge, we swing right on a concrete path crossing cultivated terraces then join the main dirt track (Wp.4 55M) to **Bar La Vista**.

Bearing left, we cross the car-park and go through the bar, stopping as long as the stomach stipulates, then take the stepped garden path at the southern end of the terrace down to a paved trail. Following the trail (S), we cross a stream then, when the trail climbs to a new house protected by a stout fence and three portly, tumultuous dogs, branch right, re-crossing the stream onto a dirt path that rejoins the main track at a ford (Wp.5 60M). Crossing the ford, we climb

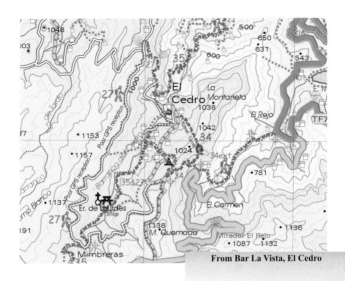

**From Bar La Vista, El Cedro**

along the main track, turning first right then first left (after the second house on the left) (Wp.6 65M) on a stepped path with blue waymarking. Ignoring all branch paths, we pass two clusters of houses before bearing left at a park-limit sign and returning to the forest.

Climbing gently to steadily between giant fern and towering laurel, we pass in front of the **Ermita de Lourdes** (Wp.7 75M) and cross a picnic area with an extraordinary little *fuente*-in-a-tree (10,000 litres of water pass through this tree every 20 minutes according to one of the park firemen), beyond which a footbridge brings us onto a stepped ascent to a broad dirt trail. Ignoring a branch to the right, we follow the left bank of the stream, re-crossing via another bridge to return to our starting point.

Unless you're staying in **San Sebastián**, this route's not practical as a day excursion, but as a commuting route between two of the island's best walking areas, it's hard to beat.

3 | 2¾ H | 9.5 km | 250m / 900m | 3*

\* in **Vallehermoso**

**Access**: bus L1, L6 or L7 to **Hayas**, bus L3, L5 or L7 from **Vallehermoso**.

**Extension**
See Walks 13, 14, & 17 for links to **Arure**, **Cercado** and **Valle Gran Rey**

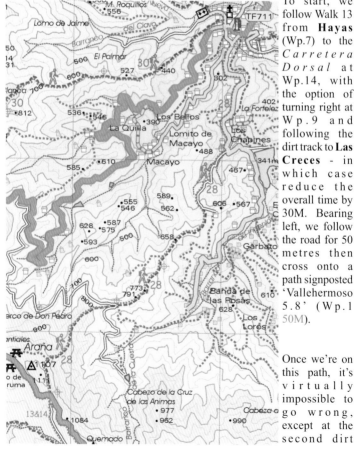

To start, we follow Walk 13 from **Hayas** (Wp.7) to the *Carretera Dorsal* at Wp.14, with the option of turning right at Wp.9 and following the dirt track to **Las Creces** - in which case reduce the overall time by 30M. Bearing left, we follow the road for 50 metres then cross onto a path signposted 'Vallehermoso 5.8' (Wp.1 50M).

Once we're on this path, it's virtually impossible to go wrong, except at the second dirt track (Wp.6). The descent is in two parts, the first dropping off the island's central spine through slightly degraded *laurisilva*, the second running along a narrow ridge cloaked in *fayal-brezal*.

After strolling along a level path through lichen-frosted laurel with fine views over **Vallehermoso**, we come to a junction signposted 'Raso de la Bruma 0.7' to the left (Wp.2 60M). Bearing right, we zigzag down onto a long north-easterly traverse, after which we wind more tightly through woods alive with the chatter and staccato cries of birds. We then come to a level ridge path (Wp.3 70M) leading across a slight rise.

Vallehermoso and Roque Cano.

Gradually emerging from the tree cover into more degraded forest, we zigzag down to the **Pista de la Meseta** at a '*Sendero Local*' signpost (Wp.4 85M).

Crossing the dirt track, we take the path for 'Los Chapines 2.5km', skirting to the east of two small peaks at the head of the ridge we follow down to **Vallehermoso**. This narrow path would soon be washed away if it wasn't for the bushes and trees underpinning it, but these are a mixed blessing as we duck and weave between hat-snatching, hair-snarling branches. Snaking along the ridge, we descend to a bald chalky dome (Wp.5 100M), where the path continues along a narrow erosion gully. 150 metres before a large outcrop of rock that resembles a recumbent dinosaur, our path drops down onto the eastern side of the ridge before winding round onto the western side and descending steeply to another '*Sendero Local*' signpost just above a dirt track (Wp.6 120M).

The signpost has been misplaced and appears to suggest we bear left on a rough path running parallel to the dirt track, which we can do, but have to rejoin the track 150 metres later. In either case, it's the track we follow all the way down to the **Barranco de Ingenio** road (Wp.7 145M) emerging opposite the **Artesania Los Roques** if you happen to be doing this route in reverse. Bearing left, we follow the road into **Vallehermoso**, arriving at the end of **Calle Triana** between the restaurant of the same name and the **Bar Garajonay** (Wp.8 165M).

**Vallehermoso**, or 'Beautiful Valley', suggests one of those anodyne gated communities they're so keen on in southern California, but as this classic circuit shows, in this instance the name is no more than a prosaic statement of fact. Warming up with a pleasant stroll along a *pista forestal*, we continue with a dramatic climb past the hamlet of **El Tión**, after which a well-graded descent brings us back to town via **Roque Cano**, the protean *roque* that dominates the entire valley.

**Stroll**
If you just want to stretch your legs in peaceful countryside, you could do worse than follow the dirt track to **Embalse de Vallehermoso** and back.

**Short Version**
Taxi to **Restaurante Roque Blanco** and do the linear descent.

**Access**: by car and bus  L3, L5 or L7

From **Bar Garajonay** in the centre of **Vallehermoso** (Wp.1 0M), we descend toward the **Carpinteria Nirgen**, bearing right behind the celebrated 'statue' playground on the tarmac lane to **Garabato**. After the first U-bend, we turn right on steps with a green railing (Wp.2 5M) climbing to cut off a long loop in the lane. Bearing right when we rejoin the lane, we ignore a branch track to the left (our return route) and continue along the lane, which soon becomes a dirt track (Wp.3 15M), climbing gently at first then, after crossing a watercourse (Wp.4 25M), more steadily. After an attractively restored house with a decorated agave-scape gateway, we see a white cabin and pale green vine terraces at the head of the valley. The 'cabin', in fact a fairly substantial house when you come to it, is the one we reach at Wp.9. A few minutes after passing a house extended with a second, wooden storey (Wp.5 40M), we see the

**Embalse de Vallehermoso** dam wall. 150 metres before the dam, 50 metres after a white water-hut topped with a solar panel, we leave the dirt track, turning sharp right on a broad rock path marked with cairns (Wp.6 50M).

The path, which is partially stepped, climbs steadily to steeply, zigzagging up a rocky spur. Shortly after crossing an abandoned concrete canal (Wp.7 55M), we see the white 'cabin'again and, a little to the north, the largely abandoned hamlet of **El Tión**. After passing a solitary palm and ancient ruin (Wp.8 70M), the spur narrows to a spine with steps cut into the rock leading up to the white 'cabin' (Wp.9 75M), a good spot for a breather, with concrete benches and great views.

Behind the house, we bear left, toward **El Tión**, on a narrow terrace path. Ignoring a minor branch doubling back on the right, we take the second turning on the right, climbing steep stone steps past a wooden electricity post to the end of a tarmac lane (Wp.10 80M). Bearing right at the Y-junction 50 metres later and ignoring all subsequent branches, we climb steeply to the small *mirador* (Wp.11 95M) below the **Restaurante Roque Blanco**. Following the main lane past the restaurant, we ignore a minor dirt track branching left and, 50 metres later, turn left onto a broader dirt track marked with cairns (Wp.12 100M).

Roque Cano

Descending along the dirt track, we get our first glimpse of **Roque Cano**, memorably described by David & Ros Brawn of Discovery Walking Guides as 'Dan Dare's Spaceship', but equally reminiscent of some Gaudiesque experiment in modernist gothic architecture. At double green gates (Wp.13 110M), we leave the dirt track, bearing left on a broad walking trail, initially running alongside a precipitous drop, happily screened by shrubs. A long, gentle descent with superb views up the 'Valley of 1001 Palms', brings us onto the first of several roughly cobbled sections remaining from the days when this was a donkey trail, some of the rocks of which are so heavily burnished they appear to have a worn ceramic surface.

We then round a corner for our first really impressive view of **Roque Cano**: spaceship, temple, or simply a very large lump of rock? 150 metres later, our trail broadens to a smooth ridge path, passing a *Monumento Natural* signpost (Wp.14 130M) and a pockmarked *roque* that would be a celebrated place of pilgrimage itself were it not dwarfed by **Cano**.

Passing below **Roque Cano**, the trail winds down onto a long exposed spur, still high above **Vallehermoso**. Ignoring occasional faint traces branching off the main, paved trail, we zigzag down, criss-crossing and finally veering away from a thick water pipe. Passing between houses on the outskirts of town (Wp.15 160M), our trail runs into a dirt track rejoining the tarmac lane of our outward route, five minutes from **Bar Garajonay**.

# 30. ERMITA DE SANTA CLARA + CHORROS DE EPINA

Ensconced in the domestic beauty of **Vallehermoso** one might suppose the entire north-west of the island is nothing but a charming bucolic. In fact, this area boasts some of the wildest landscapes in the Canaries and climbing up to the **Ermita de Santa Clara** gives us some of the best views to be had of the little visited ravines between **Arguamul** and **Alojera**. Not recommended in hot weather.

| 5 | 4H* | 14 km | 650m / 650m | ↻ | 3* |

* in **Vallehermoso**

**Strolls**
(a) **Barranco de la Era Nueva** to the threshing circle
(b) drive along the **Arguamul** dirt track to Wp.8 and walk to the *ermita* from there
(c) 30 metres above the **Bar/Restaurante Chorros de Epina** on the **Vallehermoso-Valle Gran Rey** road, just before the paved track signposted 'Chorros de Epina', bear right on a concrete slipway running into a path down to the multi-channelled spring. Drink from left to right (even spouts for women, odd for men) to win the love of your life. Thirst quenched (I offer no guarantees for the rest of it) take the steps up to the **Ermita de San Isidro** and follow the paved track back to the road.

**Short Versions**
Bus L4 or L7 to the **Epina** turn-off then do the linear descent from Wp.9 or follow the **Arguamul** dirt track to the *ermita* and do the ascent in reverse.

**Extension**
Instead of doubling back at Wp.9, stay on the **Epina**/**Alojera** road to its junction with main road, 150 metres along which we come to the **Bar/Restaurante Chorros de Epina** and the stroll.

**Access**: by car and bus 🚌 L3, L4, L5, or L7. To reach the start of the walk from the main plaza in **Vallehermoso**, on foot or by car, take the narrow street to the right of the **Bar Central** up to the **Valle Gran Rey** road. 150 metres up the road, turn right at the *Guardia Civil* barracks for the *cementerio*. Park on the cemetery access lane.

From the junction next to the barracks (Wp.1 0M), also signposted 'PR Vallehermoso-Chijeré', we follow the lane to the cemetery and turn right on a concrete ramp descending to a footbridge over the **Era Nueva** ('New Threshing Circle') stream. Ignoring all branches, we stick to the main trail, climbing to a cluster of houses (Wp.2 10M) where we bear left. Looking up to the left after the last house, we can see the **Montaña Blanca** communications mast where our descent begins. After climbing above the last house, our trail swings left (WNW) and the gradient eases. We follow this trail all the way up **Barranco de la Era Nueva** to the *ermita*. Text-phobes shut the book now!

After a long gentle climb up the valley, which is dotted with date palm and juniper (as usual in the Canaries, what Northerners are accustomed to seeing as a bush is a tree), we pass an abandoned house (Wp.3 30M), the second after the cluster at Wp.2, and the gradient steepens on a small rise above a large reservoir, 150 metres after which we reach the 'new' threshing circle (Wp.4 40M). The trail then winds into the stream bed, which it criss-crosses for the next few hundred metres. The watercourse is so densely packed with bamboo and house-leeks, it's a job to know whether you're on the left bank, right bank, or actually in it, but after a long steady climb clearly on the right bank (our left), we pass a terrace wall set with step-ladder stones, immediately after which the watercourse divides (Wp.5 55M) and we branch right, ignoring a minor path to the left. We soon leave the stream bed, climbing steadily to steeply through *fayal-brezal* and a small stand of eucalyptus, after which we bear left on a ridge below **Tesselinde** and the trail levels out alongside wooden railings (Wp.6 80M), from where we have superb views of the coast and Tenerife. We now stroll alongside **Tesselinde** to emerge on a dirt track (Wp.7 90M) 100 metres from the *Ermita*.

The track NE to **Chiguere** leads to a dramatic descent: it also leads to some of the driest land on a dry island and a dull slog up the **Playa Vallehermoso** road. So

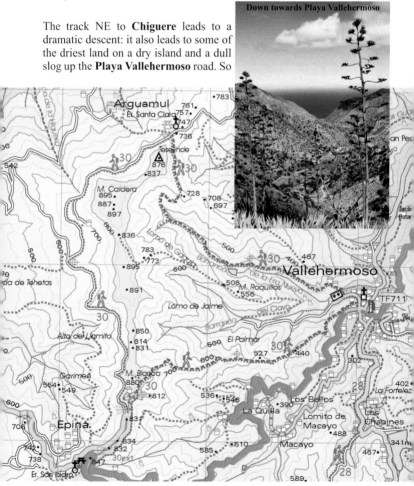

Down towards Playa Vallehermoso

having spent a little while enjoying (weather permitting) the views down toward the coast from the *ermita* and possibly taking advantage of the small *área recreativa* behind it (water available), we retrace our steps to Wp.7 and follow the dirt track (SW) all the way to the **Epina** road. (N.B. If you have an old map showing apparently more interesting routes cutting across the crest, ignore it; these routes have been abandoned and are 'interesting' in the sense that jungle warfare might be 'interesting'to a certain type of temperament.) Ignoring all branches, real or imagined, we stride along the dirt track, enjoying that usual sense of euphoria when a trail levels out after a stiff climb, as if one could walk forever. Mind you, after the turning for **Tazo** and **Arguamul** (Wp.8 120M), where the track begins its very gentle but very long climb to the road, you may feel like you are walking forever. We are saved from monotony though by consistently good views – again, weather permitting.

Finally emerging on the **Epina** road at a U-bend through a cutting (Wp.9 150M), we turn left, doubling back round **Montaña Blanca** on the lane to the communications mast. After 100 metres, the lane swings sharp left and we bear slightly right, dropping down onto a small platform leading to a broad trail following a contour line (NW). Bearing right at a Y-junction two minutes later, we descend, gradually at first then more steeply, onto what appears to be a gently sloping ridge tipped with an electricity pylon (Wp.10 175M). In fact, this ridge, which we follow down to **Vallehermoso**, is a sort of giant's stairway, along which we pass a succession of steady descents interrupted by the relatively level 'steps'of the stairway. There are no branches or path finding problems until very near the end, so the following notes are merely for pacing progress.

At the end of 'step' 2 (counting Wp.10 as Step 1) we come to a long paved stretch (Wp.11 190M). On 'Step' 3, the *fayal-brezal* that has dominated for most of the descent so far, gives way to prickly pear and agave, and the trail drops down onto the northern side of the ridge next to a large palm (Wp.12 200M), from where we can see the houses at Wp.2. Running along the last distinct 'step', the trail skirts the southern side of a spine of rough, corroded rock formations, before crossing an outcrop of rock and dwindling to a path (Wp.13 210M). The path soon brings us within sight of **Vallehermoso** and, after broadening to an intermittently paved trail again, the cemetery.

We then follow the northern side of the ridge and wind down to the first house on the outskirts of **Vallehermoso** (Wp.14 225M). Ignoring a branch path to the right, we descend directly in front of the house (it looks like we're going into the garden!), onto what appears to be a private terrace, but is in fact the end of a shallow-stepped concrete path that brings us down to the **Valle Gran Rey** road.

**To return to the main plaza**, we cross straight over onto a stepped descent.

**To return to the parking area**, we bear left and follow the road round to the start of the walk.

# 31. LAS ROSAS - HERMIGUA

For anyone wanting to explore the northern coast without the massive climbs that otherwise seem inevitable, this itinerary, using a little known crossing of the **Barranco de Lepe**, is an almost wholly pleasant introduction to the area. I say almost since the paths out of **Las Rosas** have been neglected and brambles can be a problem. Long sleeves and trousers preferable though not essential.

**Access**: by bus 🚌 L3.

The walk starts in the coach park in front of **Restaurante Las Rosas**

| Short Version |
|---|
| **Agulo - Hermigua** |

Looking north from Las Rosas

Immediately north of the coach-park (Wp.1 0M), we take a rough dirt path descending alongside the restaurant. After a steep descent we traverse a sloping sheet of rock, at the bottom of which we turn left along a terrace. Rock-hopping over the **Barranco de las Rosas** stream onto concrete steps, we cross the main road (Wp.2 10M) and follow another tiny, slimy stream for 30 metres before more steps lead to a paved track, where we bear left and start climbing.

Ignoring a branch to the north, we stay on the main track as it runs into concrete then dirt before ending in front of a private house, where we turn left on a rougher dirt track. The old path to **Agulo** branches off the first U-bend of this track, but is currently impassable due to brambles. Unless this path has obviously been cleared, we continue to the end of the dirt track (Wp.3 20M), where we bear left on a faint, partially stepped way passing under an electricity cable and climbing behind a small house. At the top of a pathless slope of bare sandy rock and soil (SE), we join a clear path (Wp.4 25M) and bear left, aiming for wooden posts carrying the same electricity cable passed after Wp.3. Crossing a small rise, we see three isolated farmsteads. Our route drops down at the first then passes below the second and above the third.

The path narrows amid young heath-trees then crosses a gully, where it suffers a brief but breachable invasion of brambles, before climbing behind the first house, which is a ruin (Wp.5 35M). Bearing left, we pass behind the house and wind down a steep, snaking descent to join the old path from the U-bend in the dirt track (Wp.6 40M). We then follow a contour line below the second, smallest house, now out of sight. The path gets clearer as it approaches the third farmhouse, which is still maintained, behind which we join Walk 32, at a makeshift signpost indicating 'Agulo' straight ahead (Wp.7 50M). From here we follow a good donkey trail down to cross the main road just before the **Agulo** tunnel, where a dirt track runs into a trail to **Agulo** cemetery (Wp.8 80M) (see Walk 32 Wps.15-17 for details).

Following the cobbled lane past the cemetery, we bear left at a Y-junction and stroll through the town centre. From the plaza between the church and *ayuntamiento*, we take **Calle del Pintor Aguiar** down towards the '**Supermercado Gama**', immediately before which, we bear left on a concrete lane with a dead-end sign. 100 metres after the **Villa Maria Apartamentos**, we turn right on a tarmac lane, at the end of which (Wp.9 100M) a rough trail, either in the process of being re-paved or simply half-finished, drops down from a banana-lift to a whitewashed house.

Turning right just behind the house, we leave the paved way, crossing a terrace, at the end of which we bear left on a steep concrete stairway (watch out for the banana skins!) down to another stretch of cobbled trail. We then pick our way across the bed of the **Barranco de Lepe** via a winding bamboo alley, at the end of which a terrace path leads to a rough stone stairway into **Lepe**. Turning left into a narrow alley, we pass a house with a ceramic 'BR' nameplate, then bear right at a bright yellow house to reach **Lepe**'s tiny village square (Wp.10 115M). From here we simply follow the tarmac lane down to **Playa de Hermigua** (swimming <u>not</u> recommended) then up to the main road (Wp.11 135M) passing en route the *bar-restaurantes* **El Piloto** and **El Faro**.

A perfect circuit provided you're not too susceptible to heights. Going straight up the cliffs behind **Agulo** and strolling along **Barranco de la Palmita**, we visit the **Garajonay Centro de Visitantes** and, more pressingly, the **Bar/Restaurante Tambur**, then take a beautifully graded donkey trail for a gentle descent that's the opposite of the ascent in more ways than one. The cliff path should not be attempted in wet or windy conditions and is not recommended for a descent.

5    3H    10 km    600m / 600m    ⟳    ⚠    4

**Access**: by bus 🚌 L3 or L5, or car. Park on the main road below Wp.1.

**Short Version**
Taxi to **Centro de Visitantes** then descend as described.

**Extension**: **Hermigua** (see Walk 31)

The walk starts on the main road at the western end of **Agulo** on steps (Wp.1 0M) climbing between **Bar La Zula** and the **Casa Aixa** clothes shop. After traversing terraces on a wall path, we cross a broad cobbled lane and continue on a paved path marked by a blue arrow. Climbing between abandoned banana terraces, we cross the main road onto a steep, cobbled path marked with a pillar-signpost for 'Agulo/La Palmita' (Wp.2 5M). The cliff path is just to the left of the orange crags that come into view as we climb.

Climbing steeply between terraces, we cross a large water pipe (Wp.3 15M) below a fluted 'pedestal' at the base of the orange crags. Winding above the pedestal, we cross scrubland and then bear left on our first vertiginous section, passing under stout black plastic water pipes (Wp.4 30M) first seen draped over the pedestal. Zigzagging steeply up the cliffs, we reach a broad ledge beside a shallow cave (Wp.5 35M) roofed with fractured rock. After traversing another broad, slightly vertiginous ledge, the path swings right, muddied by a meagre spring, then re-crosses the black pipes (Wp.6 40M). After a second shallow cave we traverse another broad ledge and join an old canal, rounding a corner to abruptly find ourselves in the spacious mouth of the **La Palmita** ravine (Wp.7 45M), within sight of the **Embalse de Agulo** dam wall. If you haven't felt like admiring the view during the ascent, bear left 50 metres later onto the natural **Mirador de Agulo**.

We now follow the cairn-dotted donkey trail climbing to the right of the dam until it runs into a rough dirt track next to another pillar-signpost (Wp.8 60M). Bearing right, we climb the dirt track to pass behind a yellow house that's been visible for the last few minutes, after which we join another, major dirt track (Wp.9 65M). Ignoring the blue arrow pointing right, we bear left for a pleasant stroll up the deepening ravine - pleasant that is, so long as you don't meet one of the dust-choked 4x4 day-tripper 'safaris' from Tenerife. Five minutes after passing between two gateway palms, we turn right on a branch dirt track (Wp.10 80M), signposted 'C.Visitantes', crossing a bridge and climbing a steep spur lined with houses. Ignoring all branches, we follow the main track till it ends at a white house (Wp.11 85M), alongside which we pick

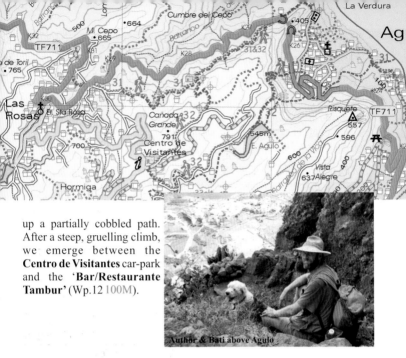

up a partially cobbled path. After a steep, gruelling climb, we emerge between the **Centro de Visitantes** car-park and the '**Bar/Restaurante Tambur**' (Wp.12 100M).

Author & Bati above Agulo

Bearing right, we follow the tarmac road between the restaurant and **Centro de Visitantes**, then branch left 50 metres later, taking the dirt track (NE) along the eastern flank of the **Cañada Grande** ridge (ignore the chain and *excepto autorizados* sign). Ignoring a branch climbing to the left, we stick to the main track, which soon dwindles to a partially cobbled donkey trail, leading to a small stand of a pine and a Y-junction (Wp.13 110M) where we bear left, as indicated by cairns. Crossing the exposed, eroded end of the ridge, we bear left again a couple of minutes later at a second Y-junction and follow a red dirt path between erosion gullies. Following the cairns, we drop down to cross the gully on the left, coming to superb views over the **Barranco de las Rosas**, and join the head of a cobbled donkey trail (Wp.14 115M).

After a steady, easy descent, we turn right above a large farmhouse at a T-junction marked with tree trunk signs for 'Las Rosas' and 'Agulo' (Wp.15 125M). Descending past the farmhouse and a modern petroglyph of a naked torso, we see our broad trail winding down to the road. After a steady descent, the trail levels out, curving round a contour below a sickly looking palm tree, where the final easy descent to the road begins - easy that is, apart from one very short vertiginous section and a distressingly big boulder that's fallen onto the path 75 metres from the road.

Crossing the road (Wp.16 155M), we ignore steps down to a shack and bear right for 30 metres to a dirt track that descends to a reservoir where it dwindles to a path. Skirting round the ridge housing the **Agulo** road tunnel, we cross another spill of massive boulders and descend onto a cobbled lane behind the cemetery (Wp.17 165M), within sight of **Agulo** church. We follow the cobbled lane to the village, turning right at a major junction to rejoin our outward route behind **Bar La Zula**.

# 33. THE HEAD OF THE TABLE AND THE FAT BACK

If you've ever looked up at some towering summit and said to yourself, "I'm going to do that, I'm going to go up there", largely because it's bigger than you and you want to be on top of it, then this is the walk for you! Climbing via the **Ermita de San Juan** to the **Cabeza de la Mesa** or 'Head of the Table', we trace a large loop round the **Barranco de Liria** then descend the **Lomo Gordo** (literally 'Fat Back') by what is probably the most spectacular path on the island. It also happens to be one of the least well known, appearing on no other maps (apart from the **Centro de Visitantes** 3D relief map) and unheard of by most people, even locals. Don't bother trying to trace it out from below: it's completely invisible and manifestly impossible. Only for experienced walkers. Possibility of vertigo. <u>Unless otherwise described, all ascents and descents are steep!</u> As always with long, difficult walks, remember, the timing excludes all breaks.

| 5 | 4½-5H* | 14 km | 750m / 750m | ↻ | ⚠ | 3 ** |

\* see **warning** below      \*\*in **Hermigua**

**Access**: by car and bus 🚌 L3 or L5. Motorists start from the long parking area south of the church in central **Hermigua**. If arriving by bus, get off at the **Museo Etnografico**.

> **Short Version/Stroll**
> **Ermita de San Juan** is a stroll in distance, but given the climb calling it a 'stroll' might contravene the Trade Descriptions Act. To turn it into something akin to a stroll, taxi up and walk down.

From the '**Boutique de Pan**' at the southern end of the parking area (Wp.1 0M), we follow the main road uphill, passing on our right the junior school and post-office, and on our left the '**Partido Popular**' office (house No.38). 30 metres after the **PP** office (the same distance north of the '**Museo Etnografico**' if arriving by bus), we leave the road, climbing west on concrete steps (Wp.2 15M). After passing several houses, the concrete gives way to dirt then resumes just before reaching the lower of the two back-roads linking the higher hamlets of **Hermigua** (Wp.3 20M). Ten metres to the right, we continue climbing on concrete steps, apparently onto a private porch, before bearing right alongside the house. Crossing the second back-road (Wp.4 30M), we take another stepped ascent, signposted 'Ayuntamiento de Hermigua, Rutas Senderos, San Juan, Acevinos', onto a path that climbs above the last houses before emerging at the end of the lane (Wp.5 45M) to the *ermita*, 50 metres to our right and well worth a visit.

The Ermita de San Juan, Teide 'floating' in the background

Either retracing our steps to Wp.5 or taking the cinder path past the *ermita* barbecue wall, we

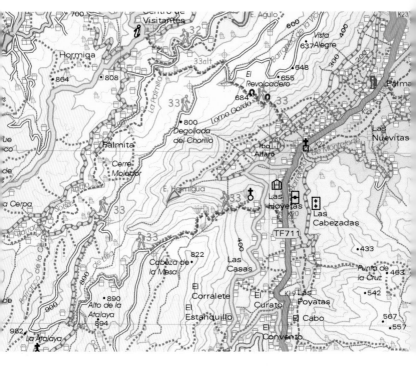

climb the narrow ridge behind the *ermita* on a clear trail that sometimes follows rough cobbles or paving, sometimes bare rock and later, dirt, but is always evident. Details are for timekeeping rather than pathfinding, though rest-stops are virtually compulsory. Passing a reservoir and stepping over a sheet of corrugated iron, we cross the **Cabeza de la Mesa** watercourse (Wp.6 60M) to a ruin.

*Climbing past the ruins.*

Zigzagging up to pass between two more ruins, we reach the first of four stretches of metal railing, at the end of which (Wp.7 70M) we ignore a faint branch to the left. Climbing past another small ruin, we come to a broader cobbled stretch. Ignoring all apparent branch paths, we stick to the main trail, passing a small railed *mirador* (Wp.8 80M) and bearing away from the **Cabeza de la Mesa** watercourse towards the **Barranco de Liria**.

At the fourth stretch of railing, we ignore an overgrown cutting to our right and follow the railings back towards the **Cabeza de la Mesa** watercourse. We then repeat the same pattern, bearing right towards the **Barranco de Liria** before swinging left back to the **Cabeza de la Mesa** watercourse, passing a small, unfinished *mirador* platform (Wp.9 95M), after which the gradient eases and our trail gradually broadens to a dirt track. 100 metres south-west of a red and grey outcrop of rock, we bear right at a cairn, leaving the dirt track and recovering the old trail (Wp.10 105M). After a steady climb on recently tailored steps, we rejoin the track (Wp.11 110M) next to another 'Ayuntamiento' signpost, just below a junction with another dirt track.

Bearing right, we stroll through *laurisilva* mixed with more domestic species such as medlar, chestnut and the pale-barked Indian Laurel often seen in Canarian town squares. The woods are wonderfully vibrant, so vital that any house left untended is soon engulfed in vegetation. Ignoring all branch paths and a major track to the right, we follow the main dirt track to the **Acevinos** lane (Wp.12 135M). Turning right, we follow the tarmac lane for a long, gentle climb, passing on our left a dirt track and a 'retevision' transmission mast, 100 metres after which, at a sharp left hand bend, we bear right on the second of two dirt tracks (Wp.13 150M).

The track winds along a ridge, gradually descending into the shallow **Barranco de la Vica**, where it doubles back to the south and a minor branch continues to the north-west (Wp.14 179M). Immediately before the junction of dirt tracks, a narrow path marked with a cairn heads west below a stand of eucalyptus (the second on the ridge). This path is your escape route if you don't like the look of the descent to **Hermigua**. Bearing right at the junction, we follow the main track down to the first sharp left bend (Wp.15 180M) where we branch right on a stepped ascent, marked by a cairn, broken railings and a signless signboard.

**On the descent**

From the top of the steps a broad trail, delineated by large stones, traverses a sandy ridge to the **Lomo Gordo** cliffs (Wp.16 185M) from where we can see the model village of **Hermigua** and its tiny toy church way below us.

If at this stage you prefer not to tackle this descent, which is daunting but not dramatically dangerous, retrace your steps to Wp.14 and take the path into the **Barranco La Palmita** to pick up Walk 32 at Wp.10.

**Warning!**
The descent is very steep, rough and vertiginous, but never suicidally dangerous (not always the case with Canarian paths!) and well within the capacity of experienced walkers. As a guideline, if you managed either the **Pared de Agulo** climb or **Barranco de Erque** descent, then you can do this descent, which is more impressive due to the greater height, but not so

vertiginous. It is all <u>walking</u> and hands, though helpful, are never essential. There's only one way to go, so don't worry about getting lost. However, a few ground rules:

**1. Go Slow**. This may sound fatuous, but take it one step at a time. Everyone must go at their own pace, which, according to your own lights, should be slow. Hence the 'cleft' walking times, which in this instance are even more subjective than usual.

**2. No Leaning**. Don't even touch let alone lean on the flimsy handrails; the wood is brittle, the concrete bases loose, and they can only give a false sense of security.

**3. Stop To Look**. Don't walk and watch at the same time. Stop to admire the view.

Descending over rocks with rough steps cemented into them, we pass a small cave and come to a declivity with a rope 'banister' (the first of several) set in the rock (Wp.17 190M-200M). At the time of writing, these ropes are in good condition and well anchored. They're not terribly useful, but it's nice to know somebody vaguely official has been this way in the recent past.

We then climb to cross a slightly vertiginous ledge, at the end of which we pass a tap (probably dry). A second slightly vertiginous stretch, is followed by a second cave (Wp.18 205M-225M), beyond which we get the distinct impression we're heading for an abyss. In fact, an easy chicane with another rope 'banister', brings us through a declivity on an increasingly clear trail. We then reach a long level northerly traverse, again slightly vertiginous as the trail narrows to a dirt path. The path broadens again as it resumes its descent, before yet another slightly vertiginous chicane brings us past a partial cave formed by an overhang and shallow recess. After a second tap (Wp.19 220M-250M), we descend through a small stand of pine and cross two abandoned canals, the second immediately above a large reservoir. Passing between the reservoir and several houses, we follow concrete steps down to the upper of the **Hermigua** back-roads (Wp.20 245M-275M). Remaining times are calculated from the minimum descent time.

Twenty metres to the left, we take the driveway down to an orange roofed house, from the gateway of which, a faint path leads down to a dirt track and the lower back-road (Wp.21 250M). Following the road north, we ignore two tempting cobbled paths apparently descending to the village but in fact going nowhere, only turning right 10 metres before a wooden sign for 'Finca La Era' and a ceramic sign for 'Casa Ico Piedra Romana' (Wp.22 260M). Stairs wind down between houses to the end of a tarmac lane, which we follow to the start of the back-road. Turning right, we descend into the village, doubtless glancing back with a 'been-there-done-that' smugness.

Short does not necessarily mean dull, at least not in the emotional sense, though things do get pretty obscure visually on this exciting circuit pioneered (with some help from the waterboard engineers!) by Ros and David Brawn of Discovery Walking Guides. It's not quite so exciting as it must have been when the tunnel was knee deep in water, but still a lot of fun. **A torch is essential**. Slight risk of claustrophobia.

\* + 20 minutes for the extension

**Access**: by car. Park in the large uneven lay-by 50 metres before a hairpin bend, 2.6 km south of the **Cruce El Rejo** junction with the TF711. Non-motorists should take a taxi to Wp.1 (ask for "Caserío del Cedro por el túnel") and use Extension (b) back to **Hermigua** or Extension (c) to the bus route.

**Stroll**
Linear route through the tunnel – branch right 30 metres after Wp.1 *por el túnel.*

**Extensions: (a)** Walk 27 **(b)** Walk 35 **(c)** see text

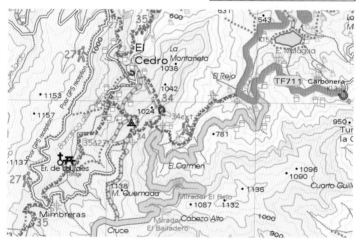

From the lay-by (Wp.1 0M) we walk up to the bend and take a broad trail, signposted 'Caserío del Cedro 0.7'. Branching left ('por el monte') after 30 metres, we climb onto a covered canal, which we follow for a few metres before bearing right on a narrow path. Immediately after a large, solitary palm tree, we swing right (Wp.2 10M) ignoring a branch to the south. Climbing steadily to steeply on a path partially stepped and paved with boulders, we curve round below a low white cliff, where more regular, tailored steps climb to a 'Parque Nacional' sign (Wp.3 20M). After a cutting flanked by tall trees, we climb more steeply through a series of tight zigzags to emerge at a bend of the **El Cedro/Mimbreras** track (Wp.4 30M).

Bearing slightly right for 'Aula de la Naturaleza/Caserío del Cedro', we follow a lovely shady path down to the nature centre car-park (Wp.5 35M).

Taking the paved trail to the right, we descend between the buildings, bearing right after solar panels and left after a row of washbasins. Following a dirt path, we cross the **El Cedro** track and descend through woods to join Walks 27 and 35 at a T-junction (Wp.6 40M). Turning right, we maintain direction (N) when the path runs into a dirt track that in turn joins the **El Cedro/Bar La Vista** track. Descending to the left, we cross a ford (Wp.7 50M), just a few minutes (not counted in the global timing) short of **Bar La Vista**, accessible via the dirt track or by crossing the wasteland on the right to take a paved trail up to the bar's terrace.

The tunnel mouth

Returning to Wp.7, we cross a stone footbridge a few metres north of the ford, beyond which someone has daubed 'Túnel' on the concrete wall shielding the entrance of an old water tunnel. Turning on our torches, we duck into the tunnel and set off into the darkness – claustrophobes and lumbago sufferers beware: as water tunnels go, this one is relatively high, but we still have to walk like Groucho Marx to avoid braining ourselves on the roof.

The tunnel curves round, so that for a while there is no light at either end, but we soon see a distant beam of sunlight as we splash through shallow puddles where the concrete has started to break up. In a little under ten minutes, we emerge at the far end and bear right, blinking in the bright sunlight, to cross a metal footbridge and rejoin our outward route, 30 metres from the road.

**Extension (C)**

If you haven't got a car, there's a path descending to the TF711. It hadn't been cleared in 2003, but was still passable. Long sleeves and trousers recommended. It starts below a large chestnut tree halfway between the hairpin bend and the lay-by (Wp.8 0M). After descending alongside cultivated terraces and passing a collapsed wall, some gymnastic twisting and turning is required to avoid being snagged on brambles. Bearing right at a small cabin, we cross a stream and pass between two houses, where the path widens to a dirt track. Rounding the bend between the houses, the track passes in front of a shrine and we turn left (Wp.9 5M) on a path descending along the left bank of a stream. The stream drops away and we climb briefly into shady woodland, laurel to the right, palm to the left. A partially cobbled stretch leads to a meagre affluent where we bear right, crossing a slab of rock before continuing on embrambled path. The path becomes drier and consequently clearer as we descend to pass a high retaining wall, within sight of the road. After descending onto a rock shelf, we cross onto the stream's right bank (Wp.10 15M) and climb slightly, ignoring an overgrown branch to the right carrying a waterpipe. We then descend past cultivated terraces and a goat pen to a lay-by on the main road (Wp.11 20M), 4 km from **Hermigua**. If you don't want to wait for the bus, it <u>should</u> be possible (I haven't tried it) to reach **San Pedro** via the dirt track 500 metres to the north signposted 'El Rejo/Lomo S. Pedro'.

Perhaps La Gomera's most famous path, and with some justification, including as it does the island's highest summit and longest waterfall, the beautiful **Barranco del Cedro**, and a forest so dense and dark it elicits a lively sympathy with gingerbread men. It's usually approached as an ascent, though why anyone would climb 1000 very steep metres to a bus-stop on a main road is beyond me. Far better hop off the bus at **Pajarito**, stroll across the **Alto de Garajonay** and let gravity do the rest. Even then it's quite energetic enough. Slight risk of vertigo between Wps. 12&13. The path between Wps. 4&8 features in the park 'Self-Guider Paths' leaflet.

**Access**: by bus L1 or L3. Drivers can park at Wp.2 and return by taxi (€20, Tel. Jose Herrera Garcia 660-292-492 or 922-880-293).

> **Stroll**
> **Las Mimbreras – Ermita de Lourdes**

From **Los Pajaritos**, the **Alajeró/Chipude** turn-off (Wp.1 0M), we take the 'Alto de Garajonay' dirt track, immediately turning right on the '**Alto de Garajonay**' walking trail. A steady climb brings us across a small rise, after which we dip down before climbing again to the signposted 'Alto de Garajonay/Contadero' T-junction (Wp.2 15M) and the end of the day's climbing!

Turning right, we descend to the summit's main dirt track (Wp.3 20M), which we follow down to the road and the parking area at **El Contadero** (Wp.4 25M), formerly a counting gate where shepherds made sure they hadn't mislaid any sheep.

Ignoring minor paths to left and right, we take the broad walking trail north. Apart from Wp.6, there's no going wrong between nere and **Las Mimbreras** as there's only the one path. All you really need to know is that the path descends steeply through successive grades of *laurisilva* to a Y-junction (Wp.6 75M) just after Self-Guider Post 13, where we bear right to cross the **Arroyo de El Cedro** stream. We then follow the right bank of the stream, crossing it once again, before joining a broader trail leading to the parking area and dirt track at **Las Mimbreras** (Wp.7 90M).

**Times between, and résumé of, the numbered Self-Guider Posts:**

1  Summit heath tree forest, the 'sponge' that absorbs the 'horizontal rain' generated by the trade winds and which accounts for as much as half the island's precipitation.
2  30M Canarian heath trees are distinct from their shrubby European counterparts, growing up to 20 metres high.
3  Wax-myrtle, the dominant species in *fayal-brezal* woodland.
4  35M *Cat's ear*, a literal translation, a colonising plant.
5  Dead, decomposing trees are essential to biodiversity and the vitality of the woodland.
6  Flat patches on the forest floor are the scars of the old charcoal burning industry.
7  (Wp.5 45M) Canarian holly, a key component of the *laurisilva* (this post was rotten and uprooted when we passed, hence the waypoint).
8  50M Dead trunks full of fungus and creepy crawly things.
9  Degraded heath forest due to natural erosion 'encouraged' by human intervention.
10  60M Former site of terraces for cultivating vegetable and cereal crops.
11  65M Epiphytic plants (e.g. moss, lichen, fern, Canarian stonecrop) = benign parasites.
12  Fungi and insects act as a mobile recycling plant.
13  Clearing for the old campsite, now home to sun-loving endemics.
14  Shoots of the *viñátigo* tree (Canarian ebony), a cousin of the avocado, get rats 'drunk'!
15  The river as artery, vital to the island's well-being.

*Fuente in a tree*

Bearing right at **Las Mimbreras**, we take the '**Ermita/Caserío de El Cedro**' path, crossing the stream and following its left bank until a second bridge (Wp.8 95M) brings us to the picnic area and *fuente*-in-a-tree at **Ermita de Lourdes**. Passing in front of the *ermita*, we ignore a path to the right and bear left, descending for '**Caserío de El Cedro**'. Sticking to the main trail above the stream, we stroll through disorderly ranks of immensely tall laurel frosted with moss and lichen.

Emerging from the woods, we ignore a branch doubling back to the left, and climb slightly to pass between the first of the **El Cedro** houses. Ignoring another branch to the left (Wp.9 110M), we pass more houses and a fine old chestnut tree, after which a paved, stepped section leads to a dirt track (Wp.10 115M). Bearing right, we follow the track round to the junction with the main **El Cedro** access track (Wp.11 120M) where we turn left for **Bar/Restaurant La Vista** (Wp.12 125M), a ramblers' institution, famous for its cress broth.

The path from the ermita to El Cedro

Taking the concrete path between the restaurant and camping area, we descend to the bottom terrace of the campsite and turn left on a cobbled path. Ignoring a branch on the right down to the river, we climb briefly toward an electricity pylon, where **Hermigua** comes into view and we start our steep, vertiginous descent into the *barranco*. Zigzagging down the cliff, we come into view of the celebrated **Salto de Agua** - Spanish water 'leaping' where everyone else's 'falls'! After what seem like interminable zigzags, we emerge at the apex of a reservoir (Wp.13 155M), the **Embalse de los Tiles**. Bearing left, we descend via a staircase in front of the dam wall, after which we follow the canalisation pipes nearly all the way to the road, though not slavishly, since the pipes occasionally drop into places ramblers aren't fitted for dropping into.

The path is obvious, except above a concrete reservoir of vivid green water (it looks like it came from a car radiator), where we ignore a branch to the right and bear left, crossing the watercourse behind the reservoir (Wp.14 170M). With superb views throughout, notably of the westernmost pinnacle of **Los Enamorados** (The Lovers), we continue alongside the pipes. After passing a tardy blue/white waymark, our route narrows to a canal path, the old canal visible under the pipes, 100 metres along which, next to a shack roofed with corrugated iron, we turn right (Wp.15 185M) leaving the pipes and crossing the stream for the penultimate time before a footbridge leads to the road below The Lovers (Wp.16 190M).

Turning right, we head into **El Convento**, from where we see the **El Curato** bus stop, just north of a bridge spanning the lower reaches of the **Cedro**. As the road swings south at a line of stone benches (Wp.17 200M) we branch left on a concrete and stone path, which we follow to the main road, 100 metres from the bus stop (Wp.18 205M).

The forested slopes of Garajonay

**See the notes on GPS use and waypoints on page 18.**

## 27. LAS MIMBRERAS

| Wp | N | W |
|---|---|---|
| 1 | 28 07.4616 | 17 13.4400 |
| 2 | 28 08.5248 | 17 13.0236 |
| 3 | 28 08.2902 | 17 12.9228 |
| 4 | 28 08.2272 | 17 12.9438 |
| 5 | 28 08.1408 | 17 12.8646 |
| 6 | 28 08.0538 | 17 12.9636 |
| 7 | 28 07.6260 | 17 13.2156 |

## 28. HAYAS - VALLEHERMOSO

| Wp | N | W |
|---|---|---|
| 1 | 28 08.6478 | 17 17.1576 |
| 2 | 28 08.8572 | 17 17.1630 |
| 3 | 28 08.9892 | 17 17.0556 |
| 4 | 28 09.1674 | 17 16.7214 |
| 5 | 28 09.3906 | 17 16.4046 |
| 6 | 28 09.7068 | 17 16.1298 |
| 7 | 28 10.0542 | 17 15.9816 |
| 8 | 28 10.6848 | 17 15.9354 |

## 29. ROQUE CANO

| Wp | N | W |
|---|---|---|
| 1 | 28 10.6836 | 17 15.9396 |
| 2 | 28 10.6992 | 17 15.8736 |
| 3 | 28 10.6146 | 17 15.6090 |
| 4 | 28 10.4076 | 17 15.4314 |
| 5 | 28 10.1892 | 17 15.3804 |
| 6 | 28 10.1424 | 17 15.1002 |
| 7 | 28 10.1070 | 17 15.0660 |
| 8 | 28 10.0818 | 17 14.9742 |
| 9 | 28 10.0116 | 17 14.9100 |
| 10 | 28 09.9888 | 17 14.7918 |
| 11 | 28 10.2186 | 17 14.4858 |
| 12 | 28 10.3530 | 17 14.4276 |
| 13 | 28 10.3284 | 17 14.7534 |
| 14 | 28 10.7208 | 17 15.2508 |
| 15 | 28 10.7040 | 17 15.8052 |

## 30. ERMITA DE SANTA CLARA & CHORROS DE EPINA

| Wp | N | W |
|---|---|---|
| 1 | 28 10.8828 | 17 16.0554 |
| 2 | 28 10.9020 | 17 16.1706 |
| 3 | 28 11.0382 | 17 16.7034 |
| 4 | 28 11.0634 | 17 16.9128 |
| 5 | 28 11.2908 | 17 17.2608 |
| 6 | 28 11.4810 | 17 17.2398 |
| 7 | 28 11.7858 | 17 17.2650 |
| 8 | 28 11.0406 | 17 17.9556 |
| 9 | 28 10.1682 | 17 17.5578 |
| 10 | 28 10.4310 | 17 17.0700 |
| 11 | 28 10.4916 | 17 16.7994 |
| 12 | 28 10.4880 | 17 16.6014 |
| 13 | 28 10.6476 | 17 16.3128 |
| 14 | 28 10.8234 | 17 16.0554 |

## 31. LAS ROSAS - HERMIGUA

| Wp | N | W |
|---|---|---|
| 1 | 28 11.2080 | 17 13.3362 |
| 2 | 28 11.1756 | 17 13.1796 |
| 3 | 28 11.0856 | 17 13.0020 |
| 4 | 28 11.0478 | 17 12.9366 |
| 5 | 28 11.0094 | 17 12.7476 |
| 6 | 28 11.0832 | 17 12.7596 |
| 7 | 28 11.1768 | 17 12.5178 |
| 8 | 28 11.5548 | 17 11.7162 |
| 9 | 28 11.3382 | 17 11.3778 |
| 10 | 28 11.1978 | 17 11.2026 |
| 11 | 28 10.4658 | 17 11.2218 |

## 32. PARED DE AGULO

| Wp | N | W |
|---|---|---|
| 1 | 28 11.2116 | 17 11.7816 |
| 2 | 28 11.2260 | 17 11.8656 |
| 3 | 28 11.2062 | 17 11.9604 |
| 4 | 28 11.1762 | 17 11.9766 |
| 5 | 28 11.1516 | 17 11.9670 |
| 6 | 28 11.1180 | 17 11.9652 |
| 7 | 28 11.0784 | 17 11.9556 |
| 8 | 28 10.8816 | 17 12.1626 |
| 9 | 28 10.8204 | 17 12.2376 |
| 10 | 28 10.5414 | 17 12.6282 |
| 11 | 28 10.5726 | 17 12.7182 |
| 12 | 28 10.6782 | 17 12.8442 |
| 13 | 28 10.9626 | 17 12.4800 |
| 14 | 28 11.1222 | 17 12.4404 |
| 15 | 28 11.1636 | 17 12.5274 |
| 16 | 28 11.5236 | 17 11.9784 |
| 17 | 28 11.5698 | 17 11.7156 |

## 33. THE HEAD OF THE TABLE AND THE FAT BACK

| Wp | N | W |
|---|---|---|
| 1 | 28 10.0728 | 17 11.7006 |
| 2 | 28 09.6450 | 17 11.9184 |
| 3 | 28 09.6714 | 17 11.9286 |
| 4 | 28 09.6840 | 17 12.0258 |
| 5 | 28 09.6834 | 17 12.1914 |
| 6 | 28 09.6522 | 17 12.3120 |
| 7 | 28 09.6318 | 17 12.3822 |
| 8 | 28 09.6552 | 17 12.4314 |
| 9 | 28 09.5718 | 17 12.4836 |
| 10 | 28 09.5112 | 17 12.6564 |
| 11 | 28 09.4458 | 17 12.7974 |
| 12 | 28 09.0222 | 17 13.3860 |
| 13 | 28 09.6456 | 17 13.0866 |
| 14 | 28 10.5306 | 17 12.3072 |
| 15 | 28 10.4172 | 17 12.2772 |
| 16 | 28 10.3320 | 17 12.1506 |
| 17 | 28 10.3110 | 17 12.0876 |
| 18 | 28 10.2834 | 17 12.0774 |
| 19 | 28 10.2612 | 17 11.9934 |
| 20 | 28 10.1268 | 17 11.9214 |
| 21 | 28 10.1136 | 17 11.8764 |
| 22 | 28 10.2636 | 17 11.6322 |

| 34. | | | 35. | | |
|---|---|---|---|---|---|
| **EL CEDRO TUNNEL** | | | **CLASSIC GARAJONAY** | | |
| Wp | N | W | Wp | N | W |
| 1 | 28 07.7640 | 17 12.6516 | 1 | 28 06.4980 | 17 14.4996 |
| 2 | 28 07.8426 | 17 12.6570 | 2 | 28 06.6636 | 17 14.6808 |
| 3 | 28 07.8462 | 17 12.6984 | 3 | 28 06.8244 | 17 14.6280 |
| 4 | 28 07.8528 | 17 12.8040 | 4 | 28 06.9540 | 17 14.5962 |
| 5 | 28 07.9392 | 17 12.8682 | 5 | 28 06.9852 | 17 14.2548 |
| 6 | 28 07.9758 | 17 12.9750 | 6 | 28 07.2648 | 17 13.5558 |
| 7 | 28 08.1366 | 17 12.8592 | 7 | 28 07.4496 | 17 13.3896 |
| 8 | 28 07.7820 | 17 12.6486 | 8 | 28 07.5756 | 17 13.2414 |
| 9 | 28 07.7466 | 17 12.5442 | 9 | 28 07.9392 | 17 13.0314 |
| 10 | 28 07.9944 | 17 12.2844 | 10 | 28 08.0538 | 17 12.9576 |
| 11 | 28 08.0478 | 17 12.1140 | 11 | 28 08.1060 | 17 12.8244 |
| | | | 12 | 28 08.2368 | 17 12.9024 |
| | | | 13 | 28 08.4810 | 17 12.6972 |
| | | | 14 | 28 08.6520 | 17 12.4662 |
| | | | 15 | 28 08.8524 | 17 12.3240 |
| | | | 16 | 28 08.8914 | 17 12.2304 |
| | | | 17 | 28 09.1098 | 17 11.9226 |
| | | | 18 | 28 09.1806 | 17 11.9526 |

This glossary contains Spanish and Canarian words found in the text (shown in *italics*) plus other local words that you may encounter.

| | | | |
|---|---|---|---|
| *abandonado* | abandoned, in poor repair | *colegio* | college, school |
| | | *comida* | food |
| *abierto* | open | *cordillera* | mountain range |
| *acampamiento* | camping | *correos* | post office |
| *acequia* | water channel | *cortijo* | farmstead |
| *aeropuerto* | airport | *costa* | coast |
| *agua* | water | *coto privado de caza* | private hunting area |
| *agua no potable* | water (not drinkable) | *Cruz Roja* | Red Cross (medical aid) |
| *agua potable* | drinking water | *cuesta* | slope |
| *alto* | high | *cueva* | cave |
| *aparcamiento* | parking | *cumbre* | summit |
| *área recreativa* | official picnic spot, usually with barbecues, toilets, water taps | *degollado* | pass |
| | | *derecha* | right (direction) |
| | | *desprendimiento* | landslide |
| *arroyo* | stream | *drago* | 'Dragon' Tree |
| *ayuntamiento* | town hall | *embalse* | reservoir |
| *bajo* | low | *ermita* | chapel |
| *barranco* | ravine | *Espacio Naturaleza Protegido* | protected area of natural beauty |
| *bocadillo* | bread roll | | |
| *bodegón* | inn | | |
| *bosque* | wood | *estación de autobus/ guagua* | bus station |
| *cabezo* | peak, summit | | |
| *cabra* | goat | *farmacia* | chemist |
| *cabrera* | goatherd | *faro* | lighthouse |
| *calle* | street | *fiesta* | holiday, celebration |
| *camí* | path or way | | |
| *camino* | trail, path, track | *finca* | farm, country house |
| *camino particular* | private road | | |
| *camino real* | old donkey trail (lit. royal road) | *fuente* | spring or source |
| | | *gasolinera* | petrol station |
| *carretera* | main road | *guagua* | bus |
| *casa* | house | *guanche* | original Canary Islands inhabitants |
| *casa forestal* | forestry house | | |
| *casa rural* | country house accommodation to let | | |
| | | *Guardia Civil* | police |
| | | *guia* | guide |
| *cascada* | waterfall | *hostal* | hostel, accommodation |
| *caserío* | hamlet, village | | |
| *cementario* | cemetry | *hoya* | depression (geological) |
| *centro salud* | health centre | | |
| *cerrado* | closed | *iglesia* | church |
| *cerveza* | beer | *información* | information |
| *choza* | shelter | *isla* | island |
| *clinica* | clinic, hospital | *izquierda* | left (direction) |

| | | | |
|---|---|---|---|
| *laurisilva* | ancient laurel forest | *pozo* | well |
| *lavadero* | laundry area (usually communal) | *prohibido el paso* | no entry |
| | | *puente* | bridge |
| *librería* | bookshop | *puerto* | port, mountain pass |
| *llano* | plain | *refugio* | refuge, shelter |
| *lluvioso* | rainy | *río* | river, stream |
| *lomo* | broad-backed ridge or spur dividing two valleys or ravines | *risco* | crag or cliff |
| | | *roque* | (a) lava fill exposed by erosion to form a broad, blunt pinnacle (b) rock |
| *malpais* | 'bad lands' wild, barren countryside | *ruta* | route |
| *mapa* | map | *salida* | exit |
| *mercado* | market | *senda* | path, track |
| *mirador* | lookout/viewing point | *sendero* | foot path |
| | | *sierra* | mountain range |
| *montaña* | mountain | *sin salida* | no through road/route |
| *nublado* | cloudy | | |
| *nueva/o* | new | *sirocco* | hot, dust-laden wind from Africa |
| *oficina de turismo* | tourist office | *tapas* | bar snacks |
| *peligroso* | danger | *tienda* | shop |
| *pensión* | guesthouse | *tipico* | traditional bar/eating place |
| *pescado* | fish | | |
| *pico* | peak | *tormentoso* | stormy |
| *picon* | black volcanic rock/sand | *torre* | tower |
| | | *torrente* | stream |
| *piscina* | swimming pool | *tubería* | water pipe |
| *pista* | dirt road/track | *valle* | valley |
| *pista (forestal)* | forest road/track | *vega* | meadow |
| *playa* | beach | *ventoso* | windy |
| *plaza* | square | *vieja/o* | old |
| *policia* | police | *zona recreativa* | recreation area |

# APPENDIX A

## USEFUL ADDRESSES & TELEPHONE NUMBERS
(when phoning from the UK, prefix these numbers with 00 34)

### TOURIST INFORMATION

For official tourist information, including exhaustive lists of accommodation in hotels, pensions, guest houses and casas rurales try the government website

www.gomera-island.com

Patronato Insular de Turismo de La Gomera
Calle Real, 4
38800 San Sebastián de La Gomera
Tel: 922 141512  922 870281     Fax: 922 140151

Oficina de Turismo de Valle Gran Rey
Calle Lepanto, s/n., La Playa
38870 Valle Gran Rey
Tel / Fax: 922 805458

Oficina de Turismo de Playa Santiago
Edif. Las Vistas, local 8 Avda. Marítima, s/n., Playa Santiago
38812 Alajeró     Tel: 922 895650          Fax: 922 895651

### ACCOMMODATION

For budget accommodation (double room €27) in good walking country, **Bar-Hotel Sonia** in **Chipude** (Tel: 922 804158 Fax: 922 804310).

For luxury accommodation, the **Parador** in **San Sebastián** (www.paradores.es), **Jardin Tecina** in **Playa Santiago** (www.jardin-tecina.com), and **Ibo Alfaro** in **Hermigua** (www.ecoturismocanarias.com/iboalfaro).

There's a plethora of agencies orchestrating private lets, but one I can recommend from personal experience is **CIT Rural** (Tel: 922 144101), notably the **Don Pedro** bungalows in **Alajeró**, which are simple, cheap (€39 per day, sleeping up to 4), clean, and well situated for walking, shopping and views. Also recommended is **Casas Canarias** offering about 30 properties across the island. 106 Savernake Road, London NW3 2JR, info@casascanarias.co.uk www.evolutionsystems.co.uk/casascanarias

Other addresses/numbers for accommodation:

**Casas Rurales**
www.ecoturismas.com          www.islarural.com
**El Serrillal** in **Hermigua**
(on the route of Walk 33)
Duplex sleeping 3          Tel: 922 265768

**El Laurel** in **El Cedro**
(on the route of Walks 27, 34, & 35)
Tel: 922 880781

A selection of accommodation:

**San Sebastián**

| | | |
|---|---|---|
| **Pension Gomera** | Tel: 922 870417 | |
| **Pension Colón** | Tel: 922 870235 | |
| **Hotel Villa Gomera** | Tel: 922 870020 | Fax: 922 870235 |
| **Apartamentos San Sebastián** | Tel: 922 871090 | |
| | manuel-artega@telefonica.es | |
| **Apartaments Quintero** | Tel: 922 141744 | Fax: 922 870922 |
| | ap-quintero@teleline.es | |

**Playa Santiago**

| | | |
|---|---|---|
| **Pension La Gaviota** | Tel: 922 895135 | Fax: 922 895031 |
| **Apartamentos Casanova** | Tel: 922 895002 | |
| **Tapahuga Apartamentos** | Tel: 922 895159 | info@tapahuga.com |

**Benchijigua**

| | |
|---|---|
| **Casas Rurales** in **Benchijigua** | Tel: & Fax: 922 144101 |

**Hermigua**

| | | |
|---|---|---|
| **Hotel Villa de Hermigua** | Tel: & Fax: 922 880246 | |
| **Apartamentos Los Telares** | Tel: 922 880781 | Fax: 922 144107 |
| **Casas Rurales Padimar** | Tel: 922 880246 | |

**Agulo**

| | |
|---|---|
| **Hotel Rural Casa de los Perez** | Tel: 922 146122 |

**Vallehermoso**

| | | |
|---|---|---|
| **Bar/Restaurante Amaya** | Tel: 922 800073 | Fax: 922 801138 |
| **Casa Bernardo** | Tel: 922 800849 | Fax: 922 800081 |
| **Hotel Triana** | Tel: 922 800528 | Fax: 922 800128 |
| **Hotel Rural Tamahuche** | 922 801176 | |
| | hoteltamahuche@agst.e.telefonica.net | |

**Valle Gran Rey**

| | | |
|---|---|---|
| **Casa Bella Cabellos** | Tel: 922 805182 | |
| **Pension La Vueltas** | Tel: 922 805216 | |
| **Pension Parada** | Tel: 922 805052 | |
| **Apartamentos Playamar** | Tel: 922 806009 | |
| **Hotel Gran Rey** | Tel: 922 805859 | Fax: 922 805651 |
| | www.hotel-granrey.com | |
| **Apartamentos Sur** | Tel: 922 805052 | |
| | casaamarilla@canaryart.net | |
| **Charco del Conde** | Tel:922 805528 | Fax: 922 805502 |
| | info@charcodelcone.com | |

## CAR & MOTORBIKE HIRE

Car rentals are plentiful and easily arranged on arrival. Motorbikes can be rented only in **Valle Gran Rey** from **Alofi Rentals**, Tel: 922 805554/805353/805802 Fax: 922 805554/805353 www.bike-center-gomera.com

## TAXIS

| | |
|---|---|
| **Cercado (Bar Maria)** | Tel: 922 804034 / 922 804167 |
| **Chipude (Bar Sonia)** | Tel: 922 804158 |
| **San Sebastián** | Tel: 922 870524 |
| **Valle Gran Rey** | Tel: 922 805058 |
| **Jose Francisco** | |
| **Correa Pinero** | Tel: 616 917062 / 922 805261 |
| **Hermigua** | Tel: 922 880047 |
| **Jose Herrera Garcia** | Tel: 660 292492 / 922 880293 |
| **Vallehermoso** | Tel: 922 800279 |
| **Agulo** | Tel: 922 801074 |
| **Playa Santiago** | Tel: 922 895022 or 922 895300 |

## EMERGENCIES

| | |
|---|---|
| General Emergencies | Tel: 112 |
| Medical emergencies | Tel: 112 |
| Guardia Civil emergency number | Tel: 062 |

# APPENDIX B

**BUS TIMETABLES**

Ask in the Tourist Office or the bus station in San Sebastián for up-to-date information on all lines and for approximate journey times to individual destinations. Bus L2 goes to the **Imada** turn-off before returning, rather than stopping at **Alajeró** as indicated on most printed timetables.

| Nº | Mon - Sat | Sun/Fiestas |
|---|---|---|
| **1** SAN SEBASTIÁN - VALLE GRAN REY | 10:10, 14:30, 18:30, 21:30 | 10:10, 18:30 |
| VALLE GRAN REY - SAN SEBASTIÁN | 05:30, 08:00, 14;00, 16:30 | 08:00, 16:30 |
| **2** SAN SEBASTIÁN - PLAYA DE SANTIAGO - ALAJERÓ | 10:10, 14:30, 18:30, 21:30 | 10:10, 18:30 |
| ALAJERÓ - PLAYA DE SANTIAGO - SAN SEBASTIÁN | 05:30, 09:00, 14:00, 16:30 | 07:45, 16:30 |
| **3** SAN SEBASTIÁN - HERMIGUA - AGULO - VALLE HERMOSOS | 10:10, 14:30, 18:30, 21:30 | 10:10, 18:30 |
| VALLEHERMOSO - AGULO - HERMIGUA - SAN SEBASTIÁN | 05:30, 08:00, 14:30, 16:30 | 08:00, 16:30 |
| **4** ALOJERA - VALLEHERMOSO | 07:00 | |
| VALLEHERMOSO - ALOJERA | 14:00 | |
| **5** SAN SEBASTIÁN - AIRPORT | 07:00, 13:00 | |
| AIRPORT - SAN SEBASTIÁN - HERMIGUA - AGULO - VALLEHERMOSO | 10:10, 17:30 | |
| **6** VALLE GRAN REY - CHIPUDE - AIRPORT | 07:00, 13:00 | |
| AIRPORT - CHIPUDE - VALLE GRAN REY | 10:10, 17:30 | |
| **7** LA DAMA - VALLEHERMOSO | 7:30 (Mon - Fri only) | |
| VALLEHERMOSO - LA DAMA | 14:00 (Mon - Fri only) | |

Ask in Tourist Offices or ferry port offices for up-to-date ferry information.

| FERRY/ ITINERARY | Daily |
|---|---|
| **GARAJONAY EXPRESS** Tel: 922 34 34 50/51    www.garajonayexpres.com | |
| LOS CRISTIANOS (Tenerife) - SAN SEBASTIÁN - PLAYA SANTIAGO - VALLE GRAN REY | 08:45, 13:55, 18:20 |
| VALLE GRAN REY - PLAYA SANTIAGO - SAN SEBASTIÁN - LOS CRISTIANOS (Tenerife) | 06:45, 10:50, 16:20 |
| PLAYA SANTIAGO - SAN SEBASTIÁN - LOS CRISTIANOS (Tenerife) | 07:15, 11:20, 16:50 |
| PLAYA SANTIAGO - VALLE GRAN REY | 10:05, 15:15, 19:40 |
| SAN SEBASTIÁN - LOS CRISTIANOS (Tenerife) | 07:35, 11:40, 17:10 |
| SAN SEBASTIÁN - PLAYA SANTIAGO - VALLE GRAN REY | 09:45, 14:55, 19:20 |
| **BENCHIJIGUA EXPRESS/BARLOVENTO\*** Tel: 902 10 01 07    www.fredolsen.es | |
| LOS CRISTIANOS (Tenerife) - SAN SEBASTIÁN | 09:00, 13:30, 17:30, 20:00\* |
| SAN SEBASTIÁN - LOS CRISTIANOS (Tenerife) | 07:15\*, 11:30, 16:30, 18:30 |
| **TRASMEDITERRANEA** Tel: 902 45 46 45 | |
| LOS CRISTIANOS (Tenerife) - SAN SEBASTIÁN | 08:30 (also at 14:00 Mon-Fri and at 19:00 Wed, Fri & Sun |
| SAN SEBASTIÁN - LOS CRISTIANOS (Tenerife) | 11:45 (also at 17:15 Mon-Fri) |

# APPENDIX C

**CYCLING ROUTES**

Bicycles can be rented in **Valle Gran Rey** www.Bike-Station-Gomera.com
(o)  principally off-road
(t)  principally on tarmac

Ⓐ  **San Sebastián – Playa Cangrejo – San Sebastián**
(linear return)                    (o)

Ⓑ  **San Sebastián – Pista de la Majona – Hermigua** (see Walk 4)
(linear one-way)                  (o)

Ⓒ  **Playa Santiago -  Playa del Medio – Playa Santiago** (see Walk 6)
(linear return)                   (o)*
***off-road at time of research, but golf development is under
construction in this area**

Ⓓ  **Playa Santiago – Ermita Guarimar – Playa Santiago**
(linear return)                    (t)

Ⓔ  **Targa – Playa Santiago** via **Altamoche** (see Walk 8)
(linear one-way)                  (o)

Ⓕ  **Alajeró – Almacigos – Alajeró**
(linear return)                    (t)

Ⓖ  **Chipude – Ermita de Nuestra Señora de Guadalupe – Chipude**
(linear return)                    (t)

Ⓗ  **Chipude – Cercado – Laguna Grande – Tajoras**
or **Garajonay – Chipude**        (loop)                    (o)

Ⓘ   **Las Hayas – Valle Gran Rey**
(linear one-way)                  (t)

Ⓙ  **La Calera – Lomo del Balo – Chele – Retamal – La Calera**
(loop)                    (t)

Ⓚ  **Epina – Alojera – Tazo – Epina**
(loop)                    (o)

Ⓛ  **Epina – Chigueré – Epina**
(linear return)                   (o)

Ⓜ  **Vallehermoso – Banda de las Rosas – Vallehermoso**
(linear return)                   (t)

Ⓝ  **Laguna Grande – Las Rosas**
(linear one-way)                  (t)

Ⓞ  **El Cedro** turn-off **– Las Mimbreras – Acevinos – Meriga -
Centro de Visitantes - Las Rosas**
(linear one-way)                  (o)

# APPENDIX D

**USEFUL WEBSITES**

**www.bike-centre-gomera.com**

www.bike-station-gomera.com

**www.cabildogomera.org**

www.candir.com

**www.canariasahora.com**

www.canary-guide.com

**www.canary-islands.com**

www.dwgwalking.co.uk

**www.culturacanaria.com**

www.ecoturismas.com

**www.ecoturismocanarias.com**

www.evolutionsystems.co.uk/
casascanarias

**www.fredolsen.es**

www.gobcan.es

**www.gomera.com**

www.gomera.net

**www.gomera.org.uk**

www.gomera-island.com

**www.gomera-travel.com**

www.guide-u.com/canarias/la-gomera

**www.islarural.com**

www.jardin-tecina.com

**www.mma.es/playas/html/p/todas/
go.htm**

www.paradores.es

**www.red2000.com/spain/
canarias/gomera**

www.spaintour.com/canarias/gomera

**www.walking.demon.co.uk**

# INDEX OF PLACE NAMES

Spending a lot of our time amongst dramatic landscapes, we appreciate the value of an accurately researched and well written walk description. Abroad in a foreign land is no place to find yourself lost and in danger. Knowing this, we operate a 'no compromise' policy to all of DWG's walking routes. We walk every route - repeatedly if necessary - to make sure that we have an accurate walk description. Then we try to write the detailed walk description in an inspirational tone so that you know how we felt on that route. We've slogged up that impossible looking ascent, marvelled at those panoramas, found paths through apparently pathless wilderness, have gratefully arrived at our destination. Its not always fun, but it has always been an adventure. Our GPS ground survey system means that we know exactly where we have been, except when there is poor GPS reception and we tell you this.

This 'no compromise' policy for our walking research has been much appreciated by users of DWG walking guides, as our post bag testifies. The result is that with a DWG guidebook you can confidently embark on the adventures it contains knowing that we have researched every route to the highest standard.

We still marvel at every 'Your guide made my holiday' letter we receive, just as we did at the first one we ever received. Bringing adventure and enjoyment to people is very pleasing, and we are very good listeners to what our readers would like to appear in a walk description. In Walk! La Gomera you will find:-

- Walking route summary including Effort, Time, Distance, Ascents/Descents, and Refreshments
- Frequent timings so that you can judge your progress against the author
- Fully detailed walk description
- Detailed map for every walking route
- GPS Waypoints (grid references) for every key point on the route
- Full GPS Waypoint lists for all walking routes
- Island map and regional Walks Locator maps
- lots of useful background information

We haven't done all this just because La Gomera is somewhere special, which it certainly is; this is our normal 'no compromise' approach to giving you everything you need in a walking guide book.

Now, go out there and enjoy it, safe in the knowledge that Charles, Jeanette and a very large old English sheepdog have been there before. There are some easy routes. There are some awesome routes. Some routes are vertiginous. With Charles Davis's excellent descriptions you will know which routes are for you, and all of them are a true adventure.

David & Ros Brawn
Directors of Discovery Walking Guides Ltd
(That's us on the cover of 35 Tenerife Walks)

## TOUR & TRAIL MAPS FOR WALKERS

Tour & Trail Maps have been developed to meet the need for accurate, up to date, maps for regions covered by Discovery Walking Guides. At the core of each T&T map design is a comprehensive ground-level survey carried out on foot and by car. The survey results are then translated into our design programme, producing a digital vector-graphic database involving the organisation of several million pieces of information across a large number of 'layers' drawn digitally within our computers.

Once a digital vector-graphic database has been established, new developments such as new roads, tracks and buildings, can be quickly incorporated into the correct 'layer' of the database. Rapid updating, combined with state of the art 'file to plate' pre-press operation enables us to produce new editions of Tour & Trail Maps quickly and efficiently.

Tour & Trail Maps have Latitude/Longitude grids and datum information making them GPS compatible. DWG walking routes are clearly highlighted, along with their GPS Waypoints where space allows.

Since 2003, all new Tour & Trail Maps have been produced on a special high density polymer as Super-Durable editions which are waterproof and super tough, giving many seasons of use in the toughest conditions and outlasting paper maps many times over.

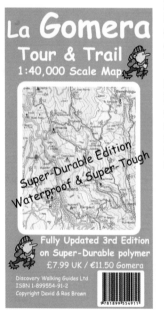

**Tour & Trail Maps** are available for:-
La Gomera
Alpujarras
Madeira
Mallorca North & Mountains
Menorca
Gran Canaria Mountains

For Tenerife, we produce a **Tenerife Walkers' Maps** title available in both paper and Super-Durable editions.